What Is *Your* Heritage and the State of Its Preservation?

Volume 4
Our Roots Run Deep

Edited by

Barry L. Stiefel

HERITAGE BOOKS
2021

HERITAGE BOOKS
AN IMPRINT OF HERITAGE BOOKS, INC.

Books, CDs, and more—Worldwide

For our listing of thousands of titles see our website
at
www.HeritageBooks.com

Published 2021 by
HERITAGE BOOKS, INC.
Publishing Division
5810 Ruatan Street
Berwyn Heights, Md. 20740

Heritage Books by the author:

What Is Your Heritage and the State of Its Preservation?
Essays on Family History Exploration from the Field

What Is Your Heritage and the State of Its Preservation?
Volume 2: Collaborations with Storyboard America

What Is Your Heritage and the State of Its Preservation?
Volume 3: Putting Theory into Practice

What Is Your Heritage and the State of Its Preservation?
Volume 4: Our Roots Run Deep

Front Cover Credit:
"Family Record", Terre-Haute, Indiana: J. M. Vickroy & Co., 1889.
Library of Congress, Prints and Photographs Division.

International Standard Book Numbers
Paperbound: 978-1-55613-278-0

Dedication

In remembrance of those who passed from Covid-19 in 2020. May their memory be a blessing.

Table of Contents

List of Figures

Introduction

By Barry L. Stiefel

During the Spring 2020 semester several students at the College of Charleston's Historic Preservation and Community Planning program participated in their Senior Seminar titled "What Is *Your* Heritage and the State of Its Preservation?". This was the fourth time this seminar topic had been taught at the College of Charleston, with previous occurrences in 2014, 2016, and 2018. Unfortunately, the outbreak of Covid-19 occurred during the Spring 2020 semester, which caused the campus to close early for public health purposes. Therefore, the students in the Spring 2020 semester completed half of the term from home, which changed the learning and writing experience compared to previous times taught.

For this class, each student had to conduct a lengthy in-depth research paper on the state of preservation of heritage sites, material objects, or traditions associated with their family's history. The assignment used genealogical and family history research in an unconventional way by elevating the assessment of ancestors beyond typical names, dates, and generational succession; so commonly found on most family trees. The students had to ask profound questions to guide their inquiry, such as "Where (as in a specific spot) did my ancestors come from?"; "What was life like for them?"; and "What cultural traditions were important for them?". In this way the researcher becomes connected with their cultural forebearers, who are contextualized within time, place, and society. Moreover, the students had to utilize and synthesize the knowledge, skills, and experiences they acquired in previous classes. The class of 2020 was also able to read and discuss the essays of their predecessors from 2018, which were published in the third edited volume of this series.[1]

Following some understanding of their family history background the students then had to investigate "What is the current state of preservation?" of these places, customs, and artifacts related to their ancestor(s). They learned how to evaluate significance of place or artifact in respect to their family history, both within a personal framework as well as larger meaning within society as a whole. In some instances, the answer was easy because a student's ancestor of study was well known to contemporary historians, and the place(s), things, or customs associated with them were being well cared for. In other instances, students focused on a more vernacular past, where detailed records were often not readily available or never existed in the first place. While some of the students were descended from famous people of the past, it became important for the students to recognize the achievements of those whose names have almost or have become forgotten; especially considering that this is where the bulk of humanity comes from. Thus, the ethical question that was postulated, if one does not investigate and advocate for the preservation of one's own history and heritage, who will? And, if not now, when? Documenting our stories was the first step, and we all have a story to share.

Since this is the fourth volume of this series of published student papers, the subtitle of *Our Roots Run Deep* for the book has been used. The reason for this is that after the past three experiments in 2014, 2016, and 2018, there is now an established tradition of investigating one's own heritage to both serve as a capstone experience within the Historic Preservation and Community Planning program and as a pedagogical tool for preparing preservation students to be better preservation advocates. Further readings on this can be found in *Genealogy and the Librarian: Perspectives on Research, Instruction, Outreach and Management,* co-edited by Carol Smallwood and Vera Gubnitskaia, where there appears the chapter "Beyond Names and Dates on a Tree: How Librarians Can Help Explore Family Heritage and Preservation."[2] More can be read about this in "The Places My Granddad Built': Using Popular Interest in Genealogy as a Pedagogical Segway for Historic Preservation," which I wrote and appears in *Human Centered Built Environment Heritage Preservation: Theory and Evidence-Based Practice*, co-edited by Jeremy C. Wells and myself.[3] This is a more dynamic, critical way to approach the fields of heritage preservation and genealogy. Because ultimately, if the preservation of cultural heritage is not in some way personal to someone, then why are we doing it? Making a twist on the National Trust for Historic Preservation's campaign for "This Place Matters," the act of preserving *must* matter as well.

Within this book are six essays volunteered by some of the students after the semester had ended, with each committing some additional time for revision and research after graduation. The essays have a geographical interest in the southern United States, with some more historical while others are contemporary and reflective of other places from an earlier time. Mackenzie Turner's *Privateers, Policemen, and Bakers, Oh My!: My Family's Immigrant History in Charleston, South Carolina* is the first chapter for the fourth volume. She has found that few people from the past make their way into the history books. Even fewer have their stories actively told today if they did not have an impact on the built environment in their own time. However, according to Turner, their stories are not less important because of this. In this chapter, Turner researched her immigrant ancestors to Charleston, South Carolina. She found that all of the ancestors she investigated had significant impacts on the city's past but are unrecognized in the city's public history narrative, and that this is likely the case for many others. This chapter argues that contributions by common folk are important because this is from where most people alive are descended, and that this sort of social history is what is needed in Charleston's public history narrative tours and sites.

In *It Takes a Village: The Long Road to Preserving a Family's History: An Archive of the Harris, Capps, Early, and Barnes Family*, by Jesse Q. Harris, the second chapter investigates federal census records and other government documents in order to piece together a history that makes the foundation for the various lineages in his family. Harris's overarching goal is to compile a record for both the paternal and maternal sides of his family, to order to identify where there are remaining gaps in understanding the past. For Harris, it is important to record family history in order to prioritized what needs to be saved and what of the past can be forgotten.

In the third chapter, Jackson Royall continues the scholarship in the Carolinas, but with a focus in the mountains, in *Stewards of the Blue Ridge Foothills.* This chapter studies the cultural tradition of hunting in the Royall family, as practiced since their beginnings in America, which was one the foremost attributes to their survival on the Southern frontier. The chapter details the lives of the men who have shaped the author, the meaning derived from remaining material culture and landscapes, and the effects of socioeconomic change across twelve generations of the family. The preservation of hunting is explored in regard to the Royall family as a case study for others in this segment of society. Royall has found that demographic decline in rural areas, poverty, inaccessibility, and climate change are contributors to the waning of the pastime, and that the number of individuals who remain able to pass on the tradition is shrinking. Aspects of individuals within the Royall lineage will be observed over generations to paint an overarching image of hunting, homesteading, and surviving in the rural South. Changes to the landscape brought new social and economic practices that altered the way those in the Royall family interacted with their surroundings, and in turn changed the meaning of hunting. The chapter concludes with recommendations for preservation actions to consider.

In the next chapter, *Raised on Religion: The Preservation of Religious Cultural Heritage of a Family*, by Martha Stegall, is explored religious cultural heritage and the continuation of religious values, beliefs, and traditions through time in a family from Virginia and Kentucky. According to Stegall, the inclusion of church and community in the preservation of records, property, and religious theology leads to the most accurate representation of the religious cultural heritage. The same practice applies to Stegall's family for the preservation of her Christian religious heritage. Through sound intangible heritage preservation practice future generations can continue the legacy of their ancestors through shared beliefs and morals.

Chapter 5 looks beyond the eastern seaboard in *Living, Learning, and Loving: A Story About Family Heritage and Preservation*, by Cara E. Quigley, with a geographic emphasis on Galveston, Texas. Quigley's approach is a study of memory, the value of memory, and how they evolve over time. Particularly as oral traditions are passed from one generation to the next in a family, it is important to remember what makes each person and generation unique. The reason for Quigley's research is to document present perspectives and memories about the past for the objective that future generations will have something tangible to reflect with since thoughts and memories are so very intangible and perishable. Quigley's chapter is her gift to family members, both present and future, as a means for memories to live on.

The last chapter is a contemporary reflection

from Maryland, looking back at a family's experience through the Holocaust in Europe, with a new life rebuilt in Israel, followed by the next generation in the United States. In *Pluznik Stories About the Holocaust*, by Rachel Pluznik, we learn about her family's life in relation to the Holocaust and contemporary Judaism in general, with her story serving as a preservation tool for others of her generation who may not have access to this kind of family history. Pluznik has found that many people of her generation (Gen Z) do not have direct, first-hand accounts on what happened during the Holocaust because there are so few remaining surviving witnesses. Moreover, the generation that witnessed the genocide and survived are unable to share their stories because it is hard to talk about and/or difficult to remember their stories properly because of age. Pluznik uses her family as an example of how memory of the Holocaust still continues and shapes the lives today of young American Jews. She wants to preserve these stories of struggle and perseverance that shaped her life and other Jews of her generation. Whether the Pluznik story helps others preserve their own history, or is used to provide a more critical outline of the events on the Holocaust overall, this chapter seeks to educate to prevent future genocide.

In closing, this sample of papers reflects the students who volunteered their research from the Spring 2020 semester. A list of the other papers is included to demonstrate the breadth and diversity of the students who took the class and decided not to publish. It is our hope – both my own as well as the students' – that our work can serve as an inspiration to others to think more comprehensively about one's own family history and heritage. To think beyond names, dates, and generational succession so that the lives of our ancestors can be better understood; to begin processes of reconciliation because of new perspectives about the past and race not previously considered; as well as to foster and promote the preservation of the places, heirlooms, and traditions we have inherited today for future generations.

List of Student Papers <u>Not</u> Published Here From 2020:

Luke Bagwell	*From Sokndal to Charleston: A History of Norwegian Emigration to the American Southeast and the Preservation of Immigrant Stories*
Savannah Burgess	*The Gift of Heritage and Southern Lineage*
Jordan Cooper	*Ruby Lee Cooper and Dorothy Odell Womack: Preserving the Cultural Heritage of Two Women Living in Mid-Late 1900s America*
Coleen Cronin	*Coleen Cronin Heritage Preservation*
Abby Gullion	*Big Stone Gap, Virginia*
Savanna Heim	*Sacrifice of Southern Lineage*
Robert Morrow	*The Unique and Innovative History in My South Carolina Heritage*
George Ronan	*Ancestry on the Avalon: A Study of My Heritage*
Olivia Rothstein	*Albert Rothstein: The Mark He Made and the Stamps He Left Behind*
Will Silcox	*The Silcox Family History in Correlation with Sullivan's Island, South Carolina*
Hampton Slagle	*The Smell of Home: More Than Just a Marsh and an Ocean Being Developed*
Jordan Yale	*Southern Oracle: The Transition from Family Residence to Historic Landmark*

Figure 0.1: The Caroline and Albert Simons Jr. Center for Historic Preservation at the College of Charleston, where the students spent a significant amount of time on their Bachelor of Arts degrees in Historic Preservation and Community Planning. Photograph by the editor.

Chapter 1: Privateers, Policemen, and Bakers, Oh My!: My Family's Immigrant History in Charleston, South Carolina

By Mackenzie Turner

In the historic heart of downtown Charleston, South Carolina thousands of tourists get a glimpse of the city's history and culture on a walking or horse drawn carriage tour. On the tour, they may hear stories of pirates as they pass the Old Exchange and Provost Dungeon that held these buccaneers. Many will marvel at the historic architecture funded and built by enslaved labor. While riding by the battery, they will hear about the historic first shots of the Civil War that occurred across the harbor. Maybe after the tour they will visit one of Charleston's many famous restaurants for a taste of "authentic" Lowcountry cuisine. Through this journey the tourists will only see a glimpse of the city's past because not everyone who lived here made their way onto the history books or guided tour scripts. What contributions did people make to the city's history that are not reflected in the built environment? Why are they left out of the public history narrative? Should they be included in the future?

My maternal grandmother's side of the family has lived in Charleston as long as anyone can remember. No one knows for sure exactly when the family first arrived in the area but no one can remember a time before we had not lived here. Most people in America can trace their heritage to immigrants from other nations and because Charleston is a port city, I found an abundance of immigrants in my family tree. Through this process I found a French privateer, an Irish policeman, and a German baker. Each of these individuals were a part of the city's history but did not leave physical impacts on the built environment. Therefore, their experiences are not as visible to those visiting the city today because there are no physical locations that represent them. Despite the lack of physical impact on the city's landscape, many have had a hand in shaping history in their own ways. The experiences of my family's immigrant ancestors to Charleston demonstrates that everyone has the ability to shape the culture of a place in a diversity of ways. However, their absence in the city's public history reveals what is preserved in public memory and what has been forgotten or left out.

For this project, I traced immigrants in my family who arrived in the United States after the American Revolution. Some members of my family, such as the McKenzies and the Milligans, lived in Charleston prior to the American Revolution. However, few documents survive about these individuals from this era and it is difficult to gather a clear image of their lives. Additionally, several other family members have no documents about their lives before the Civil War. Therefore, it is difficult to say when the first relative came to Charleston. This paper will focus on individuals who immigrated to Charleston in the nineteenth century and their contributions to the city's history and culture.

Charleston and Research Before My Family

The focus of my paper is on the city of Charleston and several works helped in giving general background information about the location but do not focus on the particular area of this paper. *Charleston! Charleston!: The History of a Southern City,* by Walter J. Fraser Jr. chronicles the city's history.[1] The work provides a general overview of the history of Charleston's history from the time of its founding to 1989. Fraser covers several aspects of the city's history in a chronological order from the close examination of a mix of primary and secondary sources. However, he does not analyze any single aspect of the city's history and does not propose any thesis about the significance of the area. I am also focusing on the city's history, but my focus is on how it pertains to my family. This paper argues for adding the significance of immigrant narratives in the larger history of Charleston.

There are also works that focus on specific areas of Charleston's history that relate to my paper. Melvin H. Jackson's work, *Privateers in Charleston: 1793-1796* focuses on the history of French privateers along the South Carolina coast in the late eighteenth century.[2] Part of my paper will also discuss this time period and this phenomenon but in a different context. I will focus on a specific person during this period. Also, in contrast to Jackson, my paper will discuss the lasting legacy of pirates and privateers in the city through public history. Similarly, W. Chris Phelps' work looks at the Civil War from the perspective of those fighting in it from Charleston.[3] This paper instead examines the viewpoint of immigrant fighters and their experiences after the war during Reconstruction. In contrast to these works, my paper adds to the field by focusing on specific subjects and their interactions with Charleston's history.

Donald M. Williams' work, *Shamrocks and Pluff Mud: A Glimpse of the Irish in the Southern City of Charleston, South Carolina,* comes the closest in similarity to my paper's argument.[4] This work discusses the history of Irish immigration to Charleston and the contributions of the Irish community to the city's history and culture. I take a similar perspective in my paper by arguing for the contributions of immigrants to Charleston's history through the lens of family history.

Alexander Bolchoz: French Privateer

As a port city, Charleston has a long history with the sea and those who make their living on the water. With this history comes a legacy of privateers and pirates who use the openness of the waters to their advantage. Because of the constantly changing nature of the sea, there is little that physically remains of those who lived their lives on it. If one digs a little deeper, they can bring the remains back to the surface once more.

My seventh-great-grandfather, Alexander Bolchoz, was a privateer for the French government in the late eighteenth and early nineteenth centuries. According to a 1795 document written by a French government official, Bolchoz was thirty-two years old at the time of the document's writing and was originally from Paris, France.[5] From this document, it can be assumed that he was born around 1763. In February of that year, France signed the Treaty of Paris, which ended the Seven Years War.[6] France lost this war on land and on sea resulting in a large loss of overseas territories.[7] After the signing of the treaty, France had 47 ships in their navy and Spain 37 ships in their navy, compared to the 111 ships of in the British navy.[8] Many of the resources in the country were drained following this war and others. From the combined past three wars, the monarchy lost 3.5 billion livres, with a third of this loss coming from the Seven Years War.[9] Despite these losses, many did not begin to question the authority of the monarchy yet. At the time of Bolchoz's birth, France continued to operate under the *ancièn regime*. This was a social, economic, and political system that divided the populace into three "estates." The members of these groups can be defined as "clerics who prayed, nobles who fought and commoners who labored."[10] The clergy made up the first estate and the aristocracy compromised the second estate. The rest of the populace remained in the third estate. Most likely my ancestor was in the third estate like the majority of France at the time. However, this estate system would not last the entirety of his life.

A few years before the official start of the French Revolution, France began to see extreme poverty and food shortages. Beginning in 1789, when Bolchoz was twenty-six years old, the wheat harvest failed and brought famine and increased economic difficulties. The cost of bread rose, causing people to spend more of their incomes on staples.[11] An unusually severe winter and flooding created an economic backdrop for the "political storm" that was about to arise. In the *ancièn regime*, the first and second estates had more political power over the third and had the power to outvote them in France's legislature. A group of Parisian men decided to challenge this arrangement in May 1789. Their frustration culminated in the Tennis Court Oath in June in which this group decided to not disband until France had a constitution that placed the power in the hands of the people rather than the monarchy.[12] The French Revolution was officially underway.

That next month, on July 14, rebels attacked the Bastille, the state prison in Paris. With this attack, Paris was officially in the hands of the rebels. In August, the new National Assembly announced the Declaration of the Rights of Man and Citizen which established the principles of a constitutional monarchy. While the political leaders were making strides in achieving their goals in the Revolution, life for the average citizen was not improving. In October, the women of Paris joined together to march on Versailles, the king's palace, to demand a change to bread costs. They broke into the palace and threatened the life of the queen. The revolution carried on with the rebels in control of the city and in October 1791 they declared the monarchy abolished. Two years later Louis XVI and Marie Antoinette were publicly executed in Paris by guillotine. They would not be the last to die at the hands of this machine. The revolution became increasingly dangerous for those near its center as the leaders became suspicious of those who could threaten its success. Soon the period known as the "Great Terror" commenced and 2,000 people died by guillotine in Paris in 1794.[13]

There are not any French records on Bolchoz's life in France other than the 1795 document claiming that he was from Paris and his approximate age. As well, the first American document concerning him also comes from this year. It is unclear how much of the French Revolution he witnessed, but the majority of the events that happened occurred in Paris where he might have lived. Perhaps he witnessed the storming of the Bastille by rebel forces, or was a part of the crowd surrounding the execution of Louis XVI. Maybe he had a mother or sister who were one of the women who marched on Versailles, and demanded an audience with the king, desperate for food. Nevertheless, his time in France during his early adulthood was likely dominated by the events surrounding the Revolution. Bolchoz lived in a Paris that was facing a great shift in political, economic, and social life. He lived at the epicenter of one of the great changes in European history. While his exact role in these changes is unrecorded, he certainly was near them. While this was a major moment in history, it is only the prelude to Bolchoz's story.

While Bolchoz's involvement with the French Revolution is unknown, the movement followed him to South Carolina. In an article published in the Charleston *City Gazette* in 1795, a French citizen related some business troubles he had with other French citizens of the city: Mege had given money and a slave to Gorlier and Nadau for a store they operated in the city with a verbal commitment that he wanted an equal share in profits. Before Mege's involvement, the only money the shop owners had were "those the citizen Alexander Bolchoz left with them."[14] The author signs the article "salut en la Patrie" and dates the month and year in the style of the revolutionaries as "9th Thermidor, 3d year of the French Republic, one and indivisible."[15] This is one of the earliest documents of Bolchoz in the United States and reveals that although he was in a new country, he was active in Charleston's French expatriate community.

In the United States, Bolchoz was a privateer for the French government. A privateer was a "privately owned vessel bearing a commission from a sovereign state that empowered her to seize declared enemies of that state on the high seas."[16] Therefore, privateers were people who were able to capture other ships that were affiliated with enemy nations because they had approval from their own nation. They received a "letter of marque and reprisal" which was the document that certified that the privateer was operating under the jurisdiction of a government. However, this method was often used as a "legal cloak for banditry on the high seas."[17] The letter of marque was the only thing that distinguished a privateer from a pirate. Even with the letter, many played on the "borders, and beyond, of outright piracy."[18] After a privateer captured another ship and reported it to their own government, the privateer could keep all property on the enemy's ship and do anything with it. For many, this aspect drove them to the occupation. Privateering was a means to make fast money. Governments had few requirements for the people they sanctioned to steal from enemy ships. Rarely were inquiries made about the character of privateers and international law requirements were hardly enforced.[19] Therefore, the occupation attracted people from many backgrounds for different intentions.

Often privateering was "a weapon of last resort" for a nation at war and Revolutionary France was at that stage of necessity. Their navy was weak from recent wars and social upheavals so they turned to privateering once more to slow further losses of overseas territories. In January 1793, the revolution in France became a global maritime conflict that would last for more than two decades. Charleston became the main American dépôt for the French privateers in this conflict, with the height of French privateering spanning from 1794 to 1795. Charlestonians welcomed the French privateers because of the French Huguenot descendants in the city and a general favor for the French Revolutionary cause.[20] It was in this environment that Bolchoz spent the majority of his time as a privateer.

In 1795, a minister in the French government named Jean-Francois Theric wrote a memorial to the privateers who served France while in South Carolina, that "history's pencil will trace with approbation their accomplishments and will shield them from the oblivion."[21] Through their actions, Theric claims that these privateers have made the "French name redoubtable in the New World."[22] In the document, he named the privateers that were, in his view, the most important in their effort against the British, their archenemies.[23] One of the people mentioned is Bolchoz, stating that at the time he was thirty-two years old, commanded several vessels, including Bolchoz's flagship schooner, *la Parisienne*. Theric wrote about an event where Bolchoz captured an English brig and sent it to Charleston. Bolchoz then engaged in a fight with another ship but he was forced to retreat, but succeeded in "[killing] many of the people on the enemy vessel and had inflicted an extraordinary amount of damage."[24] In the battle, Bolchoz lost a gunner, a sailor, his chief officer had his right arm shot off, and he himself was seriously wounded in the arm. Because of this battle and others, Theric granted Bolchoz the "Brevet and Grade of Lieutenant de Vaisseau."[25] Theric's statement shows that Bolchoz was a privateer for the French government and reached great success in this position.

Not all of Bolchoz's privateering endeavors took place off of Charleston's shores. The same year of his commendation for his actions in South Carolina, he overtook the Spanish post of La Balize in present-day Mississippi. On the October 13, 1795, Bolchoz's ship, *La*

Parisienne, took possession of La Balize at the mouth of the Mississippi.[26] When the ship first arrived at the post, it sailed under the Spanish flag instead of the French. Because it carried the Spanish flag, the people stationed at the post went out to meet the ship. They were made prisoner and Bolchoz and his crew of forty-five men remained at the post until October 21. On that day, news reached the French privateers that Spanish reinforcements were coming up the river from New Orleans to recapture the post. After this news, the French left on *La Parisienne* after "having destroyed everything they could."[27] This was not Bolchoz's last interaction with the Spanish. According to a Philadelphia newspaper reporting on maritime news in Charleston, in early November Bolchoz returned to the city after an eventful cruise. During this expedition he "captured a Spanish brig and two Spanish sch'rs, one of which mounts 10 guns."[28] He also spoke to another Spanish ship which "informed him that England had declared war against Spain."[29] According to Melvin H. Jackson, this was the last time that Bolchoz appeared in the Charleston harbor with his ship the *La Parisienne*.[30] This ship was known as one of the best privateer ships because she was "remarkably fast and manned by Desperadoes of all Nations.'"[31] However, the ship *La Parisienne* was not the only one in Bolchoz's fleet.

In March 1797, Bolchoz captured the ship, *Nancy*, off the South Carolina coast.[32] John and Robert Donnellson owned the ship with Captain Cunningham in charge of sailing it. According to this newspaper, Bolchoz used the ship "*Le Polly*, alias the *Coffee Mill*."[33] However, another newspaper that reprinted the same event referred to the ship as "*Paulina*."[34] Nevertheless, Bolchoz captured the *Nancy* after a two hour chase. Following this, the two ships sailed to St. Augustine, Florida where Bolchoz tried to unload and sell the cargo on the *Nancy*. The ship carried "salt, 50 hogsheads of earthen ware, 30 boxes glass ware, 30 calks ironmongery."[35] The governor at the port refused to allow them entry because "he had no authority for the condemnation of American vessels."[36] Since he could not unload his prize in St. Augustine, Bolchoz sailed for Cape Francois. Captain Cunningham did not want to go near St. Domingue, so he offered to ransom the ship for $1,500.[37] Bolchoz accepted the ransom and the ship *Nancy,* then sailed to Savannah once again under Captain Cunningham.[38]

One of the articles reporting this event goes on to explain the backstory behind the nickname *Coffee Mill* for the ship *Le Polly.* According to this source, the year before the ship appeared in Virginia as a merchant ship. After a trip to Cape Francois, it came back to the United States with guns and ammunition which made it look like a war vessel. An official seized the ship so that it could be inspected and Bolchoz was charged and put on trial. The newspaper claims that they do not know what charges were made against them but that in the process of the investigation a "Coffee Machine" was found on the ship. Therefore, the ship earned the nickname the *Coffee Mill* because it "turns out to grind American property."[39] Bolchoz was acquitted of the charges but the nickname stuck to the ship.

In the same article on the *Nancy* incident and the nickname *Coffee Mill*, the author notes that Bolchoz's family "now resides in said city," referring to Charleston.[40] While this article is from 1797, there are documents from Philadelphia a few years later that suggest Bolchoz and his family lived there. There is a baptismal record from St. Joseph's Catholic Church for a Julia Bolchoz on July 24, 1800. Julia's parents are listed as "Alexander Bolchoz and his wife Mary Capé."[41] Bolchoz appears in a list of letters notice at the post office for Philadelphia in October 1801.[42] This could be another Alexander Bolchoz considering that the 1797 article said his family lived in Charleston. However, it is also possible he lived in Philadelphia for these years and then moved back to Charleston. This is supported by a marriage announcement for Julia Bolchoz and Peter Mahler in Charleston in December of 1820.[43] Julia would have been about twenty at her marriage and unfortunately a widow at twenty-one. Just before their first wedding anniversary, another notice appeared in the *City Gazette* asking for those with debts against Peter Mahler's estate to come forth to settle them because he had passed away.[44]

If it is the same Alexander Bolchoz in the Old St. Joseph record, then his religion was Catholicism. At the beginning of the French Revolution, the clergy sympathized with the Revolutionaries.[45] In 1794, leaders decided to "de-Christianize" the country by replacing the calendar with a new system and closing almost every church in France.[46] Around the time that Bolchoz began his life in the United States, France's government no longer supported Catholicism. The continued religious practice in the United States signifies that Bolchoz may not have agreed with the revolutionary leaders in this regard. Unfortunately, attitudes towards Catholics did not improve with the move to Charleston. While South Carolina supported religious tolerance, few Catholics lived in the city in its early days because of the association of that faith with the Spanish who threatened the colony.[47] This may be why Julia Bolchoz was married by a Lutheran reverend, John Bachman, instead of a Catholic priest.[48] However, this oppression did not last long and did not stop all members of the Bolchoz family from practicing Catholicism. Alexander Bolchoz's grandson and my fifth great-grandfather, Theodore Bolchoz, held his funeral at the Catholic St. Patrick Church in Charleston.[49] Catholicism continued to be the faith of Alexander Bolchoz's descendants unto the present, as a headline from 1998 proclaims, "Bolchoz name equals Catholicism in Charleston."[50] In the face of persecution in France and the United States, the Bolchozs were able to maintain their religious practices. Their story reveals that immigrants to Charleston in the early nineteenth-century faced religious persecution in their home countries and continued to face similar adversity in the United States, but persevered to maintain their heritage for future generations.

While settled in Charleston, Bolchoz continued to be a privateer. He may have moved from Philadelphia to Charleston around 1803 because this is one of the first documents of him living in the city outside of the 1797 *Nancy* newspaper article.[51] The next document from Charleston is a city directory listing for Bolchoz from 1806. Bolchoz was listed as a captain living at 17 Guignard Street.[52] In 1809, Bolchoz was listed as a mariner living at 108 Meeting Street.[53] Between these directory entries, he captained a ship sometimes referred two as the *Two Brothers* or the *Three Brothers*.[54]

Listed in the 1810 U.S. Census is the Bolchoz household in Charleston. According to this document, there were two white males under the age of ten, one white man under the age of forty-five, one white female under the age of ten, and one white female between the age of twenty-six to forty-four. In total, there are six household members.[55] Although Bolchoz was about forty-seven at this time, so the man listed as age forty-five may be himself. The white female under age ten was likely Julia Bolchoz, and the female aged twenty-six to forty-four could be Mary Capé, who was listed as Julia's mother in the baptismal record. The two boys could be other children of Alexander and Mary. Most likely, one of these boys was Peter Alexander Bolchoz, who is my ancestor. It is unsure when Alexander Bolchoz passed away. There is a death certificate but, it states that the deceased is a black female infant.[56] Most likely this is a death certificate for one of his enslaved children.

Figure 1.1: An exact prospect of Charlestown, the metropolis of the province of South Carolina from the late eighteenth century. Library of Congress Prints and Photographs Division.

While in Charleston and the surrounding area, Bolchoz contributed to the sea-faring legacy of the city. Charleston since its founding has been a port for trade and business, often attracting figures such as pirates and privateers. The legacy of the former is celebrated in many tours. Today, a visitor to Charleston can choose from a walking tour led by people dressed as "pirates" with parrot companions to boot, a pirate harbor tour on board a boat, and even a pirate ghost tour.[57] However, the majority of these tours focus on the "Golden Age of Pirating" and figures such as Blackbeard and Stead Bonnet. Currently, there is not a tour or museum dedicated to the history of French privateering in Charleston. By examining Bolchoz's life, it is apparent that privateering was a large part of Charlestonian sea life in the early nineteenth century and that immigrants had a major role in this phenomenon. The prevalence of pirate themed tours today proves in part the importance of these figures in the city's historic and cultural heritage. In being a privateer, Bolchoz serves an important role in local history and in the foundations of the city's culture. He has an equal role in this history with Blackbeard, Stead Bonnet, and Anne Bonny. However, he is not mentioned in these tours because he did not achieve the same level of fame as these figures in his lifetime. His story reveals that simply sometimes people get left out of the history books because they were ordinary people. His personal erasure out of the public history narrative on pirating in Charleston is not due to bias, but due to his lack of fame and direct impacts on the landscape. His story is important but not to the public at large.

John Cassidy: Irish Policeman

The Civil War was a major event in Charleston's history because the war itself started in the city's harbor. It was a war over the practice of slavery and states' rights (vs. federal powers) that tore the nation in two. New to the United States, immigrants had the difficult question of what side to take? For immigrants to Charleston during the Civil War, this was a complex question to answer. John Cassidy, my fifth great-grandfather, immigrated to the United States from Ireland and became a police officer and later a Confederate soldier. On his death certificate, Cassidy is listed as sixty-three years and eleven months old in April 1880.[58] This places his birth around May 1816. There is a baptismal record for a John Cassidy in June of 1816 in Armagh, Ireland.[59] This John Cassidy's parents are listed as Edward Cassidy and Margaret McAnalon.[60] It is not entirely clear if this is the John Cassidy who immigrated to Charleston, but this is close to his age. Cassidy never filed naturalization papers and therefore it is unclear when he left Ireland. His death certificate says he lived in the city for forty-three years, putting the year of his immigration at 1837, when he was twenty-one years old.[61] John Cassidy represents an early phase in Irish immigration to the United States.

Immigrants had been coming to Charleston from Ireland since the colonial period. During this time, immigrants arrived directly from Ireland to Charleston, but at the beginning of the nineteenth century many came to the city indirectly by first stopping at other ports.[62] New York City became the major port for Irish immigrants with 202 Irish ships landing in their harbor between 1815 and 1819. However, the number of immigrants to travel directly from Europe to Charleston between 1819 and 1861 were fewer than 2,000.[63] There are no records on where Cassidy first landed in the United States, but it was likely outside of South Carolina.

Irish immigrants to Charleston in the antebellum period often filled a labor niche caused by the end the importation of slaves from Africa. Immigrants worked construction jobs such as digging the canal in Columbia. Following the Charleston fire of 1838, the cheap labor of Irish immigrants was needed to rebuild damaged structures. The Irish population continued to grow in the early nineteenth-century and lead to the creation of the Roman Catholic Diocese in Charleston in 1820 led by the Irish-born Bishop John England. A few years later, the next wave of Irish immigrants came to the United States because of the Potato Famine (1845-1849) where over a million people died from starvation. Another million Irish left their country for economic opportunity elsewhere.[64] Assuming John Cassidy's death certificate is accurate, he left Ireland a decade before the famine, but he may have left behind family who suffered. Despite leaving in times of desperation, Irish immigrants soon made a home for themselves in Charleston with their own cultural traditions.

Irish immigrants in Charleston celebrated their heritage through St. Patrick's Day. Starting in 1749, Irish people in Charleston celebrated the feast day of St. Patrick on March 17. People gathered for a large dinner and entertainment, usually accompanied by music. In the nineteenth century, with the arrival of more immigrants, the celebrations began to change, evolving from a nighttime dinner to an all-day affair. Around 1823, the Irish Volunteers organized a parade through Charleston. The following year, the St. Patrick's Benevolent Society joined as another major organizer of the event. The parade would begin early in the day and make its way towards one of the Catholic churches on the peninsula where participants would then celebrate Mass. After the Mass, the parade continued the processional out of the church to a point of dismissal. Later in the day, many would hold private dinners to continue the celebration. In the years before the Civil War, the St. Patrick's Day parade continued to grow in size. With the influx of immigrants from the Potato Famine, was a rise of Irish citizen organizations that participated in the parades. This led to the development of two separate parades, one that marched to the St. John the Baptist Cathedral on Broad Street and the other to St. Patrick's church.[65] It is likely that Cassidy and his family partook in these parades with the Irish community in Charleston.

The first record of John Cassidy in the United States is the 1860 Federal Census. According to this document, he is a forty-one year-old police sergeant born in Ireland. There are several other people living with him. First is his wife, Frances Cassidy, who is thirty-six at the time of the census and was born in South Carolina. Together, they have seven children ranging in age from twenty years old to one and a half.[66] Frances' maiden name was Munday and she also came from a family of immigrants. Her parents were Thomas and Mary Loyd Munday. They were married on January 23, 1817 in Manchester, England.[67] The marriage certificate lists Thomas Munday's profession as a "wheel-wright."[68] In the United States, he continued a similar line of work as a "coach maker" according to the 1819 Charleston city directory.[69] Mary Munday also owned a dry goods store on King Street according to a city directory from the 1830s.[70] However, this is the end of their story and there are few other records on the Mondays. The Cassidy family continued to live in Charleston and was about to witness one of the biggest moments in the city's history.

In December 1860, representatives from across South Carolina met in Columbia to make an important decision in the State's history. They later moved to Charleston to make the official declaration on December 20, where South Carolina would secede from the United States. The first active outbreaks of war would not come until April 12, 1861, when the Confederate army began firing on Union-controlled Fort Sumter. The fighting continued into the next day when the Union surrendered.[71] This was the beginning of what became a four year war that many Cassidy family members joined.

Alexander Duncan was the first in the Cassidy family to enlist in the Confederate Army. He married John Cassidy's eldest daughter, Mary Eileen, and was an immigrant from Scotland.[72] Duncan enlisted in February 1862 and joined the 27th South Carolina Regiment in Company C.[73] This regiment, also known as Gaillard's Regiment, was the division that all of the Cassidy men became involved with in the war. Lt. Col. Peter Gaillard led this regiment starting in March 1862.[74] The majority the soldiers in this regiment were from Charleston.[75] A few months after Duncan enlisted, Dennis Cassidy also joined Gaillard's Regiment. Dennis was John Cassidy's only son and was about twenty years-old at the time of his enlistment as a private on April 7, 1862, nearly a year after the fighting started.[76] Both Duncan and Cassidy fought in the early battles of the Civil War.

The Battle of Secessionville took place on James Island in June 1862. The Union troops were beginning to move north from their position on Hilton Head Island. Members of Gaillard's Regiment, including Alexander Duncan and Dennis Cassidy, fought in the battle. The fight continued for several weeks and ended in favor of the Confederates, but with severe losses. There were nine casualties from the Confederate side and many wounded.[77] Among the wounded was Duncan. The extent of his injuries is unknown but he did apply for a pension because of his injuries, with Dennis Cassidy acting as a witness.[78] The regiment was severely diminished after the battle from injuries and disease leading to a call for more participants that led to John Cassidy joining the group.

John Cassidy joined Gaillard's Regiment sometime in the latter half of 1862. According to W. Chris Phelps, sixty men joined the Charleston Battalion, Gaillard's Regiment, between August and December of 1862. Among these men was "forty-five-year old John Cassidy, an Irish-born policeman."[79] He entered company F and served in the rank of corporal for the entirety of the war.[80] Although he appears to have enlisted, Cassidy may not have morally agreed with the Confederacy's cause. Before he enlisted, in April 1862, the *Charleston Mercury* published a petition calling for State delegates to convene and reconsider their decision to secede. Those who signed the petition wanted South Carolina to rejoin the Union and leave the Confederacy. They did not state why they wanted South Carolina to join the Union, only that they wished to once more be under the "rightful operation of the Constitution."[81] Included in the list of names is "John Cassidy" and "Chas R Cassidy," possibly his brother. It is impossible to know Cassidy's personal opinions or why he joined the Confederacy after signing this petition but nonetheless the family felt the full effects of the war and actively participated in it. After three more years, the war ended and the Cassidy family faced Reconstruction Charleston together.

Before and after the Civil War, John Cassidy worked as a police officer in Charleston. In the 1860 city directory, John Cassidy and a C. Cassidy are listed as police sergeants living on Burns Lane.[82] After the Civil War, the 1867 city directory and the 1870 U.S. Census both list John Cassidy as working as a policeman.[83] The police force in Charleston began as an elected position called the "constable." These individuals were responsible for responding to concerned citizens and enforcing city ordinances. This was an unpaid position, but constables did divide the profit from fees and fines collected for crimes amongst themselves.[84] The police force grew during the nineteenth century to include a chief, two captains, six lieutenants, four orderly sergeants, eight street sergeants, and one hundred fifty privates by the 1850s.[85] During Reconstruction, African American men were allowed to join the police ranks for; however, they were unable to achieve the same success as white policemen due to prejudices and injustices.

In 1870, Cassidy rose in the police ranks to the position of second lieutenant. The previous lieutenant resigned and the city council met to elect a new second lieutenant. The mayor at the time believed that "all men were born equal" and that the "claims of the colored race to a representation should not be ignored."[86] He submitted his candidate for the office, William M. Viney, who was African American. Unfortunately, the council voted "12 nays to 3 ayes" and Viney was not elected to the office. Then the other, white, candidates were named for the office with John Cassidy among them. After the first vote, Cassidy was in the lead with six votes but the council decided to vote again to ensure that he had the majority. On the second vote, Cassidy received nine votes and therefore won the office of second lieutenant.[87] Cassidy was apparently popular in this position as soon after his election several of his fellow officers presented him with a "handsome saddle and bridle." In response, Cassidy gave a "short and appropriate address."[88] Cassidy would continue in this position until the mid-1870s when he then became first lieutenant of police.[89] Even though slavery was abolished after the Civil War, African Americans still faced oppression in many areas of life and Jim Crow, and my ancestor did nothing to stop this systematic oppression.

Following the end of the Civil War, the plantation-based economic structure in the Lowcountry came to an end and a new industry gradually took its place. Shortly after the war, advancements in science discovered that phosphate was a primary ingredient in commercial grade fertilizers.[90] Former "planters" converted their plantations to phosphate mines and others established fertilizer factories on Charleston's "Neck", and industrial area.[91] The Cassidy family was a part of this transformation of the Lowcountry landscape. In the 1880 U.S. Census, Alexander Duncan and his brother John Duncan both worked at a local phosphate mill. At the turn of the twentieth century, Dennis Cassidy also worked in phosphate mining outside of the city.[92] The Cassidy family began to find their footing in the changing environment of Reconstruction Charleston.

John Cassidy and other members of his family played a role in one of the most transformative events in Charleston's history. The Civil War was a major moment in the history of the city for better or worse. As the site of the first shots and several battles, the Cassidy family witnessed this crucial moment and participated in it. Today, tourists continue to visit the city for its role in the war. Sites like Fort Sumter tell the history of the war and Charleston's experience with it.[93] John Cassidy's experience in the city is an example of Irish immigrant life in the Civil War era South and during the Reconstruction period. His story shows that immigrants and their families were active in the war, even if they may not have totally agreed with the cause. Their stories can be seen today in part in these tours of Civil War sites. They may not be mentioned by name but visitors can understand people like them in these tours. Their legacies are preserved in part by these sites but the rest of their story is left behind in the dust.

Albin Eissbrückner: German Baker

Food is an important part of life and has a history of its own. Different parts of the world have their own cuisines passed down from one generation to the next. Each family has their own recipes and traditions associated with food. In Charleston, food is a defining element of the city's culture. Albin Eissbrückner, my third great-grandfather, immigrated to Charleston from Hannover, Germany. In December 1917, the Federal Bureau of Investigation interviewed Eissbrückner because he was a German alien living in Charleston. In this document, Eissbrückner detailed his life and how he arrived in the United States.[94] He stated that he was born in 1865 and came to the United States in 1883, arriving at Baltimore, Maryland. He left behind a sister and father in Germany, but his brother came separately and lived in Brooklyn, New York. Eissbrückner was interviewed because he never submitted papers to become a naturalized citizen. He stated he never did because no one asked him to and he "did not want to get mixed up in politics."[95] It is unclear if he ever became a naturalized citizen, but Eissbrückner continued to live in Charleston.

Throughout his life in Charleston, Eissbrückner worked as a baker. The earliest record of Eissbrückner in the city is from the 1884 city directory. He is listed as a baker for E. Albrecht and continued in this position until 1887.[96] In the 1910 U.S. Census, he states his occupation more specifically as a "bread baker;"[97] although my great-grandmother, Dorothy Priester, remembers him making gingerbread cookies especially for her.[98] In the nineteenth and twentieth centuries, the majority of the working class' diet was bread. Bread and other baked goods were a quick and affordable alternative to full course meals. All varieties of bread such as sourdough, pumpernickel, or rye were the first items a working class person reached for on the dinner table.[99] In rural areas, people baked their own bread for daily consumption, but people in urban areas depended on outside bakeries, especially the working class who did not have the time, money, or space to bake their own bread. Purchasing bread from a local bakery was often their only option. In the latter half of the nineteenth century, there were roughly over 7,000 bakeries in the United States. The majority of these businesses had four or fewer employees, often functioning as a family business.[100] Being a baker was a profession that Eissbrückner would hold for the entirety of his life, supplying the working class of Charleston with the main part of their diets.

During the 1890s, Eissbrückner married Mattie Holphy who was also from an immigrant background. It is unclear who Mattie's father was but she lived with her mother Mary Petermann and her second husband, Jacob Bertocci for the majority of her life. Mary Petermann's father, John H. Petermann, was also an immigrant from Germany. He arrived in New York on February 17, 1848 from Osterholz with his brother Diedrick and sister Bertha.[101] All three siblings stated their intent to live in Charleston. Once there, John H. Petermann worked as a grocer, eventually starting J.H. Petermann and Sons grocery. In 1886, John H. and his son John W. established the grocery at 182 East Bay Street.[102]

According to the 1900 U.S. Census, Jacob Bertocci came to the United States in 1875 from Italy, and he married Mary Petermann two years later. In all of his city directory listings, Jacob Bertocci is listed as owning a restaurant. From 1896 to approximately 1901, this restaurant was at 185 East Bay Street and from 1901 to 1908 it was located at 13 Vendue Range.[103] According to what my great-grandmother was told about the restaurant, it was "the best Italian restaurant in Charleston." [104] Around this time, restaurants were growing in popularity across the United States from high end dining to smaller, neighborhood establishments. Many immigrants operated restaurants out of their own homes in order to make a living.[105]

Figure 1.2: Albin Eissbruckner with Dorothy Priester Vonder Leith. Photograph in the personal collection of the author.

The Eissbrückner and Bertocci families both lived at 185 East Bay Street for several years together. Several children of the two families share names and the Bertocci family appears as godparents to the Eissbrückner children in baptismal records. For example, Jacob and Mary Petermann Bertocci had a daughter named Jennie and the Eissbrückner family also named one of their daughters Jennie. Jennie Bertocci was also the godmother of Jennie Eissbrückner according to her baptismal record.[106] The two families worked together to survive and provide for each other, like many other families in the city.

The Eissbrückner family was involved in various organizations across Charleston and had several friends in the city. Soon after arriving in Charleston, Albin became a member of the "Charleston Turnverein." According to an 1885 advertisement, they held a masquerade ball and Albin was in charge of selling tickets to the event.[107] Meanwhile, Mattie Eissbrückner was involved with an organization called the "Maple Grove." In 1906, she donated a cake as a prize during one of their fundraising dances.[108] In 1908, she served as a chair in organizing a masquerade ball for the organization.[109] Albin also appears to have had musical talents in addition to culinary. He was the leader of the Maener Chor Eintracht and competed at the Convention of the South Atlantic League of German Societies and Singers when it came to Charleston. He was quoted in the newspaper as saying his singers would be "the best."[110] The Eissbrückner family also found friends another family in Charleston, the Heitmanns. According to the 1910 U.S. Census, Fredrick and Lilly Heitmann were born in South Carolina but had parents from Germany.[111] They attended several of the Heitmann's parties, including Lauretta Heitmann's seventh birthday. Ottalie and Elsie Eissbrückner each won special prizes from the party games.[112] The immigrant family was able to find a community in a new place.

While they made friends and found a community in Charleston, the Eissbrückner family faced several tragedies. They lost three infant daughters in three years. Dorothea, Wilemena, and Jennie all passed as young children in 1895, 1896, and 1897 respectively.[113] A few months after Jennie's death, my second great-grandmother was born and was also named Jennie, possibly in honor of the passed infant.[114] In 1912, Mattie Holphy passed away from severe anemia and muscle weakness.[115] This may have been why Albin Eissbrückner applied Albin Jr. and Herman Eissbrückner to the Charleston Orphan House three years later. Both of the boys were rejected from the Orphan House, meaning that they were not accepted and remained with the family.[116] The eldest three children pitched in to help the family through these times by working outside of the house. In the 1920 census, Marie worked at a printing company, and both Jennie and Elsie worked at the "asbestos factory."[117] Their experiences were universal for those living at the turn of the twentieth century. Many lost children to disease or poverty. Their experiences, good and bad, were similar to those around them.

The structure at 185 East Bay Street is significant to my family because it is where they lived for an extended period of time and ran their business in a similar capacity to its use today. Today, the structure at 185 East Bay Street is three stories high and five bays wide on the upper two stories. It is a brick structure with brick ornamentation on the cornice. The windows on the second and third floors are decorated with an ornament that appears to be stucco and are shaped in three parts. The first floor is entirely covered in windows and has Classically inspired pilasters as decoration.[118] The restaurant there today, Magnolias, opened in 1990 by Tom Parsell. Executive chef, Don Drake has been the main creative force behind the restaurant since 1991. Tom Parsell claims that the site of the restaurant was the original site of Charleston's Customs House built in 1739.[119] The restaurant bills itself as "upscale" southern cuisine that "[paved] the way for restaurants in Charleston."[120] This is in contrast to the restaurant my family owned in this space, which were European ethnic. Their establishment was likely less known and catered to the working class of Charleston instead of the upper classes. The transformation of this space reflects the changing needs and priorities of the area.

Albin Eissbrückner and his family represent the influence of immigrant cuisine on Charleston's landscape at the turn of the twentieth-century and the absence of this culture on the landscape today. Charleston is famous for its culinary scene and hosts events like the Wine and Food festival every year.[121] However, signs of the Italian and German immigrant cuisine that was once housed at 185 East Bay Street no longer remain. This speaks to the difficulties of preserving an intangible heritage. It is difficult to preserve a history that is experiential. While battles and great moments in history are also physical experiences, they can be understood through text. Food is best understood through preparation and consumption. When recipes no longer remain it is difficult to recreate these moments. Nonetheless, the traditions of the Eissbrückner and Bertocci families speaks to the interactions of nineteenth century immigrants what types of cuisines are popular in Charleston today.

Conclusion

My family's addition to the tour guide narratives would make the public history of Charleston more inclusive of everyday people and more applicable to the personal heritage of the everyday person, as a case study.

I am not arguing for the specific adoption of my personal family's heritage into public history tours per se, but that more narratives about everyday working people from differing backgrounds should be included in the public arena of Charleston's history but my family's history is not the only one that should be included. Indeed, with the example of the Eissbrückner and Bertocci families, the experience of the past could even be smelled and tasted through heritage cuisine. In the end, these stories have significance only to me and my family because of our connections to these individuals. Countless other individuals made similar intangible contributions of equal significance to Charleston's history and culture and my family's history represents one chapter in that much longer book. Each of my ancestors came to Charleston and were able to impact the city in intangible ways. However, despite their contributions to Charleston's history, their lives have significance only because of their legacy in my life and therefore it is solely my job to preserve them.

Chapter 2: It Takes a Village: The Long Road to Preserving a Family's History: An Archive of the Harris, Capps, Early, and Barnes Family

By Jesse Q. Harris

In George Lucas' *Star Wars* canon, there exists a mantra: "There is no emotion, there is peace. There is no ignorance; there is knowledge. There is no passion; there is serenity. There is no chaos; there is harmony. There is no death; there is the Force."[1] The line of the mantra that always resonates with me is "there is no ignorance, there is knowledge." Despite this being the product of a fictional world, it has always been my belief that if we fail to learn, we fail to grow. In failing to grow, we remain ignorant. Thus, to avoid ignorance, we must thirst for knowledge. In this thirst for knowledge, I intend to discover my family's heritage and the state of its preservation. In researching my family history, I have found a plethora of statistical data. Mostly through the federal census records and other government documents, I have begun to piece together a history that makes the foundation for my family. My overarching goal is to compile a record for both the paternal and maternal sides of my family, giving a broad look at the surnames, my relationship to them, and the history related to it. I first plan to detail what has been lost and found, explore the good and bad of my family's past, then look at changes that have occurred where my ancestors lived. Finally, I plan to emphasize the importance of recording family history as accurately as possible; especially what of the past needs to be saved and what is acceptable to forget.

The Name of Harris

The surname Harris is a very common one. Although there is disagreement on when the surname first appears, there is a consensus that it generally means "Son of Harry." [2] Despite disagreement about where the name first appears, the most common suggestion is England and Wales, due to the number of kings named Harry.[3] Among the different variations of Harris are Herice, De Heriz, Herez, Heris, Harries, Harrys, Harryss, Haries, Haris, and many others.[4] Later, we see a move of the Harris surname from England and Wales over to Ireland, and then North America in the eighteenth century.[5] As for heraldry and coat of arms, there are at least thirty-seven different coat of arms attributed to members of the Harris family.[6] Heraldry is a type of practice of tracing genealogies through symbols, usually armorial insignia.[7] The principal part of heraldry is the coat of arms, which initially used the hereditary symbols to establish the identity of soldiers on the battlefield.[8] Heraldry eventually evolved into denoting family descent, adoption, alliance, property ownership, and profession.[9] The reason for discussing my family's coat of arms is that much of the history I have discovered is technical and gives no sense of identity. Heraldry and the coat of arms have consistently appeared as an elite status symbol.[10] However, there is an underlying emphasis on identity.[11] While my ancestral past remains shrouded in mystery, seeking out my family's coat of arms is almost like trying to find my identity. By connecting with it, I can take pride in my family. Some genealogists consider heraldry as an aid.[12] It is important to note that in places like Great Britain, the coat of arms is taken seriously enough that casual display of it without accurate tracing of one's lineage is illegal.[13] To be able to display a coat of arms, a person needs to have first traced their family's history back to the source. Additionally, anyone who wishes to display a coat of arms may only use the exact one their ancestor used.[14]

A coat of arms consists of the surface and the space inside called the field, or charge.[15] The field then typically has a color, which is grouped with metals and furs, and together they are called tinctures. Sometimes a coat of arms field will consist of two colors, also called counterchanged. Partition lines are any that divide the field, called Right and Straight lines. The field, or charge, is either proper or common, ordinary or sub-ordinary. Outside of the charge, there are sometimes different symbols or even a motto.[16] These symbols include a helmet, mantling, wreaths, crests, and supporters. Sometimes marks of cadency are present. Marks of cadency are additions to a coat of arms that indicate to whom the arms belong to, whether it be the firstborn heir or someone further in descent. The Harris Coat of Arms varies from person to person, but many contain recurring colors and images.[17] The shield commonly was either azure (blue), sable (black), argent (silver or white), or yellow/gold and contained either three crescent moons or three hedgehogs.[18] The azure (blue) represented loyalty and truth.[19] It was also devoted to the figure of the Virgin Mary. The sable (black) represented constancy or grief. The argent (silver or white) represented peace and sincerity. The yellow or gold represented generosity and, for some, the elevation of the mind. Hedgehogs are attributed to the families of Harris and its variations.[20] Most sources stated that the hedgehog stood for being a provident, or timely provider.[21] The crescent moon stood for one who has been honored by their sovereign.[22] As for my line of descent, I was able to go as far back as the nineteenth century on my paternal side. Three members of the Harris family from North Carolina came to Georgia in the early 1800s, Thompson Harris, Hampton Harris, and Frances Harris.[23]

The Harris Family

Thompson Harris III was born c.1784 in North Carolina.[24] History relayed through *Pioneers of Wiregrass Georgia* places the Harris family in Burke County, Georgia, where the marriage of Thompson Harris III and Nancy Ursery occurred sometime around 1808.[25] Thompson would have been twenty-four years old at the time, and Nancy around fifteen years old.[26] The earliest record shows a Thompson Harris in the 1820 U.S. Census for Gwinnett County, Georgia, but it is unclear if this is my ancestor Thompson Harris III or not.[27] Before 1850, only the head of the household was named.[28] All other household members were merely counted. After marrying Nancy Ursery in Burke County, the Harris family moved to several different counties between 1825 and 1860, all within at least one-hundred miles from each other.[29] *Pioneers of*

Wiregrass Georgia states that Thompson Harris III and his family lived in Appling County for several years after 1825. The census records for 1830 and 1840 both have a Thompson Harris listed as living in Appling County.[30] Sometime between 1840 and 1850, Nancy Ursery passed away around the age of forty-eight.[31] The 1850 Census lists Thompson Harris III and his family in Ware County, Georgia.[32] Ware County was formed from Appling County in 1824.[33] The 1850 census record gives the first look at the individuals in the Harris family. It gives the dwelling number and the family number (if it was applicable), names, age, sex, race, and occupation of household members, the value of any owned real estate, as well as if adults were married, attended school, and had any physical or mental illnesses.[34]

The *Pioneers of Wiregrass Georgia* says that Thompson was skilled with his hands, making chairs, household items, and other various odds and ends.[35] According to the U.S. Census Bureau, census takers were required during the 1850 census to insert the specific profession, occupation, or trade that any free individual over the age of fifteen performed.[36] The available copy for the 1850 census is faded, but looking closely, you can just make out "Chair Maker" next to Thompson Harris.[37] The *Pioneers of Wiregrass Georgia* states that Thompson Harris and his sons William, George, and Stogner and son-in-law Joseph L. Morgan all moved to Lowndes County, Georgia sometime between 1840 and 1850.[38] However, census records only have Thompson Harris and his family living in Ware and Appling Counties, both of which sit beside each other.[39] The distance between each makes it more likely that Thompson Harris and his family lived only in Ware and Appling counties.[40]

Sometime during the 1850s, Thompson remarried, this time to Lavinia West. Thompson was in his sixties, and Lavinia in her forties. Lavinia had three daughters from a previous marriage, Sally, Mary, and Lavinia.[41] I could not find any records on Sally and Mary after the 1850 census. At the time of the 1860 census, Thompson was about seventy-five years old. The census lists his occupation as 'Wheel Right.' There were no records I could find of Thompson Harris' work; however, according to information provided by Colonial Williamsburg, a wheelwright was a strenuous job.[42] For a wheelwright to produce a wheel, it took the skills, strength, and ingenuity of both a blacksmith and a carpenter.[43] The *Pioneers of Wiregrass Georgia* states, incorrectly, that Thompson Harris died sometime around 1866.[44] However, his name appears along with the elder Lavinia's in the 1870 census. Lavinia is listed by her nickname Viney, and the child that Thompson and the elder Lavinia had together, Elias, is also listed. There are currently no records that indicate that Thompson Harris III took part in the Civil War and because of his advanced age, it is most likely that he did not. It is unclear exactly when Thompson and Lavinia Harris passed away, but they do not show up again in the 1880 U.S. Census nor in their children's households either. It can be assumed then that they both died sometime between the 1870 census and the 1880 census: Thompson Harris III, around ninety years old and Lavinia almost seventy.[45]

Together, Thompson Harris III, Nancy Ursery, and Lavinia West had an estimated nine children. Out of those nine, my ancestry continued through George W. Harris.[46] George was born in Appling County, Georgia, around 1818 to Thompson Harris III and Nancy Ursery. George lived in Georgia, and family tradition states that he was a blacksmith and wheelwright, taking after his father. Together, George Harris and his father Thompson Harris III are said to have constructed covered bridges throughout Georgia, Alabama, and Tennessee.[47] Currently, I have found no records to verify this in any of the named states, instead. In the 1860 U.S. Census, George Harris is listed as being a blacksmith. Sometime around 1840, George Harris married Julia Ann Westberry, the daughter of a local Baptist Minister, Moses Westberry. George was in his early twenties, and Julia would have been approaching her twentieth birthday. George Harris is recorded as having served in the Civil War for the Confederate States.[48] According to compiled family history, George Harris enlisted as a Private in the fall of 1862, as a member of the 3rd Cavalry Battalion.[49] He, along with his unit, served on the Georgia coast, scouting and patrolling. George Harris survived the war, passing away sometime around 1894 in Echols County, Georgia, in his seventies. Julia Ann Harris lived almost another decade, receiving a widow's pension for Confederate soldiers and eventually passing away on April 26, 1910, in Berrien County, Georgia, at the age of ninety.[50]

Together, George and Julia Harris are known to have had at least ten children. Their second oldest child, James "Jim" Harris, is the next link in my chain. Born February 16, 1844 in Lowndes County, Georgia, James Harris was the second oldest.[51] Unlike his predecessors, James Harris worked as a farmer for most of his life, only stopping to fight on the side of the Confederates in the Civil War.[52] At the age of seventeen, James Harris served as a private in Company I of the 4th Georgia Cavalry. Although a record has not yet been found to verify this, the unit is said to have merged with James' father's unit, and they fought together under the commands of Lieutenant Colonel Duncan L. Clinch and Major John L. Harris.[53] By the time the war ended, James was almost twenty-one years old. James Harris married Mary Alice Stone sometime around 1865 at twenty-one years old, and Mary Alice being seventeen. From family records, "Grand Pa Jim" was a very wealthy man in the 1920s.[54] James Harris grew cotton, sugarcane, and made molasses. Using a wagon drawn by mules, James Harris carried his product to Savannah to sell, a distance of almost 200 miles.[55] Along with growing crops, James Harris also raised hogs and cattle. It is recorded that in his later years, James Harris sold his farm and moved to Adel County, Georgia. The house "was a nice frame house with six rooms, a nice yard, and a barn where he kept a nice horse and buggy."[56] Currently, the location of the house, or the land where the house was, is unknown. James Harris continued living in Georgia up until his death, sometime around 1930.[57] According to family records, Mary Alice Stone died within six weeks of James.[58] James Harris was close to eighty-six years old at the time of his death, and Mary Alice Stone was eighty-two.

Among the seven children had by James and Mary Alice Harris, we next follow William Henry Harris, born March 18, 1881, in Cook County, Georgia. There is less detail to William Harris's life than previous ancestors. William Harris married Rhena Irene Griner on October 5, 1901, and both were about the same age. Despite living through both World War I and World War II, there are no records of William Harris serving in either. William Harris worked as a farmer for the majority of his life. He eventually passed away on March 8, 1961, at the age of seventy-nine. Rhena Irene Harris passed away on April 15, 1969, at age eighty-seven.

Arthur Clarence was one of six children born to Rhena Irene and William Harris. Arthur Clarence was born on November 6, 1904, in Berrien County, Georgia.[59] By the time of World War I, Arthur Clarence was fourteen years old. Although there are no records that show that he took part in World War II, Arthur Clarence's information is on a World War II draft card from 1940. According to records written down by Arthur Clarence's widow, Susie Louise Conner, she and Arthur were married on February 21, 1925. Arthur was twenty-one years old, and Susie Louise, seventeen. Together, they had three children, Clarence Gordon Harris, Henry Randall Harris, and Carolyn Anne Harris. The family moved from Georgia to Kannapolis, North Carolina, on September 12, 1940.[60] It is interesting to note that these records verify the census and draft card from 1940. The census places the family in Georgia, and the draft card places the family in

North Carolina. Susie Louise Conner continued writing that she and Arthur came to Kannapolis and that they both worked at Cannon Mills for six years.[61] The draft card also verifies this. Eventually, Arthur Clarence began doing pastoral work, becoming a reverend and serving as a pastor for twenty-five years. Arthur Clarence Harris died on June 3, 1969, at sixty-four years of age, leaving Susie Louise Conner a widow. Arthur Clarence Harris left her a car and a mobile home, but very little money. Susie Louise Conner went back to work at the age of sixty-one so that she would have social security for support. She passed away on January 20, 2008, at ninety-nine years of age.[62]

Henry Randall Harris was the second out of three children born to Arthur Clarence Harris and Susie Louise Conner. He was also my grandfather. Born on November 23, 1928, Henry Randall Harris grew up in Cook County, Georgia. Along with his siblings, the Harris family moved to Kannapolis, North Carolina, in late 1940. Henry Randall is recorded as submitting for the draft, and after that, all records stop. Henry Randall Harris never finished high school. Eventually, he married Anna Laura Capps around 1950, Henry being twenty-two and Anna, eighteen. The couple lived in Johnston County, North Carolina. On September 1, 1951, they had their first child, Arthur Phillip Harris, my father. On April 13, 1963, their second child, Sherry Jelynn Harris, was born. Sherry died in a car crash on January 15, 1988, at twenty-four years of age. Henry Randall Harris and Anna Laura Capps continued to live in Johnston County, North Carolina, for the remainder of Henry Randall's life.

On February 8, 2010, Henry Randall Harris passed away at the age of 81. Anna Laura Capps continues to live by herself in their trailer home in Johnston County, North Carolina.[63]

Arthur Phillip Harris was born on September 1, 1951. He grew up in Smithfield, Johnston County, North Carolina and finished high school at age twenty-one. His first marriage was to Kathy, but the couple soon divorced. Arthur remarried Theressa Starr Hall, where my half-brother, Randall Phillip Harris, was born on November 9, 1976. Arthur and Theressa divorced sometime soon after. Seven years later, Arthur Phillip Harris met Martha Early Barnes, and after a short period of dating, the two were married on September 9, 1983, in Pitt County, North Carolina. Arthur was thirty-two and Martha, twenty-eight. Arthur Harris eventually finished college with the help of Martha Barnes' parents, and then went to work for Datex-Ohmeda, a producer, manufacturer, and supplier of anesthesia equipment that was bought out by General Electric in 2003. Starting as a field service engineer, Arthur Phillip Harris was responsible for the maintenance and repair of anesthesia machines around Pitt County, North Carolina. On May 21, 1992, Arthur Phillip and Martha had their first child, Jesse Quentin Harris (me). On July 7, 1993, they had their second child, my brother Timothy Davis Harris.[64]

In 2005, Arthur and Martha separated, and in 2007 they officially divorced. In 2008, Arthur remarried for a fourth time, to Miriam Katherine Vandiford, or Kathy, as she likes to be called. Arthur was fifty-six years old, and Kathy, fifty-one. Kathy is the widow of a man named Garry Eugene

Shaw, with two children, Garry Jason Shaw, and Lindsay Nichole Shaw. Garry Eugene Shaw passed away the year before, in 2007, at age fifty-one. Around 2015, Kathy and Arthur moved from Bear Grass, North Carolina to Winterville, North Carolina, where they currently live in retirement.[65]

The Name of Capps

The Capps surname is an ancient one, first appearing in the eleventh century, almost four hundred years before the appearance of the Harris surname. There are many claims as to what the name stands for or means. It most likely is a variant of Capp or the respelling of the German Kappus, a metonymic occupational name for a cabbage grower. Less likely, Capps may have represented those in a cap, or hat, making occupation, being derived from the Old English "Caep." The least likely is that it was a locational name for those who lived near or at the chapel. Variations of the Capps surname include Capes, Cape, Capper, Capps, and many more. There were at least three coat of arms for the Capps family, consisting of azure, gold or yellow, argent, sable, or gules (red) as colors and contained either antelopes, escallops, or trefoils. Gules (red) represented military fortitude and magnanimity, or generosity. Gules is also considered the martyr's color. The escallop shell signified those who had made long journeys to far off countries, who had borne significant naval command, or those who had gained great victories. The trefoil represented perpetuity or the idea that "the just man shall never wither." The heraldic antelope is not the same as an antelope found in nature, the heraldic version having the body of a stag, the tail of a lion, serrated horns, and a small tusk at the end of its snout.[66] I could not find a meaning for the original heraldic antelope, and the only other available meanings I could find were for the natural antelope, which is not what is referred to in *The General Armory of England, Scotland, Ireland, and Wales*.

The Capps Family

The line of descent from the Capps starts with a man named Littleton Capps. There are currently no records verifying Littleton Capps's birth date, but according to census records, Littleton Capps was born sometime around 1806. Between 1806 and 1830, there are currently no records that reference Littleton Capps except for his marriage to Zylphia Price on May 12, 1827, Littleton being twenty-one and Zylphia, twenty-three. While Littleton Capps' name appears in both the 1830 and 1840 census records, it is not until the 1850 census that we get a picture of the Capps family itself. Littleton Capps and Zylphia Price had at least nine children by 1850. Littleton Capps is listed as being a chain maker, and three of his sons are listed as laborers, most likely working for their father.[67] Blacksmithing is the broad occupation that would include chain making as a skill; however, it is unclear if Littleton Capps was a blacksmith or specialized in chain making. Chain making was an established industry in Britain, but I could find no reference to chain making as an industry in America during the nineteenth century, other than jewelry chains.[68] It is unlikely that Littleton Capps was a jewelry chain maker, mostly because at the next census record, he is listed as being a farmer. Currently, there is no indication that Littleton Capps participated in the Civil War. It is unclear exactly when Littleton Capps died, but both Littleton Capps and Zylphia Price are listed in the 1880 census as being boarders in Elevation, Johnston County, North Carolina and sick with dropsy.[69] Dropsy was a term used to describe the swelling of soft tissues due to the accumulation of excess water. Dropsy is a broad term, so it is a mystery as to what exactly they were afflicted with, but Littleton's name does not appear in records again.[70] Littleton Capps most likely died sometime between 1880 and 1899. He would have been between seventy-four and ninety-three years of age. Zylphia Price appears in the census once more, in the year 1900. She is listed as being widowed and living with her daughter, Mary Frances Capps Byrd. No date could be found for her death, but she does not appear again in available records. Zylphia likely died between 1901 and 1910.[71] Zylphia Price would have been between ninety-seven and one-hundred and six years old.

According to census records, Littleton Capps and Zylphia Price had a total of eleven children. One of their sons, George William Capps, is where the line continues. George William Capps was born April 2, 1845 in Johnston County, North Carolina. George Capps continued to live in Johnston County for most of his life, marrying Betsy Hawkins Byrd on October 22, 1871. George was twenty-six, and Betsy, thirty years old. U.S. Census records show that George Capps was a farmer. There is a record of a George W. Capps who enlisted on the Confederate side of the war, but it is unclear if this is the same George William Capps or not. George and Betsy both lived until 1922, Betsy dying on December 14 and George on December 23. Betsy was eighty-one at the time of her death and George, seventy-seven.[72]

George Capps and Betsy Byrd had a total of eight children together. Junius Preston Capps is where my line next continues, who was born on June 10, 1885, in North Carolina. Although there is no birth record currently available, he was likely born in Johnston County, being that each member of this Capps line can be traced back to Johnston County. Junius Capps is listed as a farm laborer in the 1900 U.S. Census. On August 2, 1902, Junius Capps married Laura Mollie Johnson, Junius being seventeen years of age and Laura, sixteen. Junius Capps had several jobs throughout his life. After farm laborer, in the 1920 U.S. Census, he is listed as working at a sawmill. By 1940, he is listed as working in furniture repair.[73]

Junius Capps and Laura Johnson had at least six children. Their second son, Jessie Asbier Capps, is where the line continues next. Jessie Asbier Capps was born September 20, 1906, in Johnston County, North Carolina. From census records, Jessie Capps was recorded as being a cloth baler around 1940. I could find no marriage certificate, but Jessie Capps married Elizabeth Adcock, most likely around 1930, based on the dates their children were born. Jessie would have been around twenty-three, and Elizabeth, eighteen years old. According to Jessie's death index, he worked as a carpenter in construction. Elizabeth died on February 17, 1990, at age seventy-eight. Jessie lived seven more years, passing away on January 4, 1997, age ninety.[74]

From available records, Jessie Asbier Capps and Elizabeth Adcock had three children, one of these being Anna Laura Capps, my grandmother. I have been unable to find much information on her. Anna Laura Capps was born on January 19, 1932, in Johnston, North Carolina. According to my father, Anna dropped out of high school but went back to get her GED. Anna Capps married Henry Harris around 1950, Henry being twenty-two, and Anna, eighteen. In 1951, they had their first child Arthur Harris, my father; followed by Sherry Harris born in 1963. Collectively with her ancestors, the Capps family has lived in Johnston County, North Carolina, for around 220 years.[75]

The Name of Early

The surname Early has at least two primary sources. The first is from the translation of the Gaelic "Ó Mocháin," or other variations that generally mean "early rising."[76] From English, it can come from habitational names or the Old English nickname for "manly" or "noble." Variations of Early include Earley, Earlie, Erlegh, Erley, Earle, and others. There is no coat of arms that I could find that went with the surname Early; however, the spelling "Earle" had at least ten different coat of arms. The reoccurring elements within these coats were the colors gules (red), argent (white/silver), yellow/gold, and sable (black) and contained either dolphins, escallops, or lions.[77] The lion represented deathless courage. The dolphin represented the animal itself, believed to be an "affectionate fish, fond of music."[78]

The Early Family

My line of descent begins with James Early, starting in 1850 where he is forty-five years old and married to Priscila, who is thirty-three. Assuming that their oldest child listed, Sumner, was the firstborn and born after James and Priscila were married, James and Priscila were most likely married in the mid 1830s. James would have been around thirty years old, and Priscila would have been about eighteen. James Early is listed as a farmer, with land worth $150.[79] There is no precise death date for either James or Priscila and I could find no mention of them in later census records.

James and Priscila's son William Jefferson Early is the only source that verifies their existence. He also happens to be the next in the line of descent. William Jefferson Early was born around 1837 in North Carolina. Like many of my family members, no full records exist until 1850. William Early is listed in the 1850 census along with his siblings and parents. From documents obtained from a later descendant, William J. Early enlisted in Company G-32nd Regiment of North Carolina on April 1, 1862 at the rank of Sergeant, for the Civil War.[80] Through records obtained from Ancestry and Fold3, William was a prisoner of war for an entire year, captured in the Battle of the Wilderness in Virginia, in May 1864, and was released on June 16, 1865. After the Civil War, William married Susan Ann Dudley around 1866.[81] William was twenty-nine and Susan was seventeen years old. William is listed as being a farmer in 1870, 1880, and 1900 census records. It is unclear exactly when William passed away, but it was most likely sometime before 1910, as Susan appears in the 1910 U.S. Census as widowed. William would have been around seventy-three years old.[82] Susan Ann lived for sixteen more years, dying at age seventy-seven on April 27, 1927.

William and Susan had at least six children, the next in the line of descent being their son Julius Jefferson Early. Julius Jefferson Early was born around 1867 in Hertford County, North Carolina. Julius Early grew up in Hertford County, working on his father's farm as a young man. On April 10, 1892, Julius married Robanna Rovena Newsome.[83] Both Julius and Robanna were twenty-five years old.

Figure 2.1: Map of Hertford and parts of Northampton and Bertie Counties, North Carolina, surveyed under the direction of A.H. Campbell, 1863. Library of Congress Geography and Map Division.

Julius worked as a mechanic, according to the 1900 U.S. Census. Currently, there is no available death certificate for Julius; however, he does not appear in the 1910 U.S. Census. It is estimated that he died sometime around 1908 at the age of forty-one.[84] Robanna lived for forty-three more years, working as a dressmaker until retiring at some point between 1920 and 1930. Robanna passed away on December 11, 1951, in Hertford County at age eighty-five.[85]

Julius Jefferson Early and Robanna Rovena Newsome had four children, the next in the line of descent being Alvah Early. Alvah Early was born June 5, 1895, in Aulander, Bertie County, North Carolina. During his youth, Alvah helped support his widowed mother and three brothers by barbering. He attended public school in Aulander and then attended Wake Forest University as a law student. On June 1, 1919, Alvah Early married Josephine Quentin Lassiter. Alvah was twenty-three, and Josephine was twenty-two. Two years later, on April 1, 1921, their only child Emily Rose Early was born. Alvah Early passed the State Bar exam in 1924. He became a licensed lawyer practicing law in Dunn, North Carolina, before opening his own law office in Ahoskie, Hertford County, North Carolina, in 1925. Later, Alvah became a trust officer of the Farmers-Atlantic Bank. In 1927, Alvah Early was elected mayor of Ahoskie, serving until 1930 when he was elected clerk of Court of Hertford County, serving until February 1, 1941.

Sometime in between 1925 and 1940, Alvah researched his grandfather, William Jefferson Early, discovering that he was a Sergeant in Company G-

32nd Regiment. After working for the campaign for the election of Clyde R. Hoey for governor of North Carolina in 1936, Governor Hoey appointed Alvah as president of the North Carolina Railroad from Goldsboro to Charlotte.[86] Also in 1936, Alvah was the first president of the Hertford County Young Democrats and was elected as a delegate to the National Democratic Convention in Philadelphia. Alvah attended the convention again in 1940 when Franklin D. Roosevelt was nominated for the third time. On February 1, 1941, Senator Bob R. Reynolds appointed Alvah as chief field deputy with the Internal Revenue Service, which he served in until August 12, 1943. Sometime between 1940 and 1943, Alvah Early was elected President of the Hertford County Bar Association, serving as so up until his death. In October 1943, Alvah was appointed by Representative Herbert C. Bonner as postmaster, serving until June 30, 1965, when he was mandatorily required to retire at the age of seventy. Over those twenty years, Alvah saw stamp sales rise from $20,000 to over $100,000 a year. At the start of Alvah's tenure as postmaster, Ahoskie had a second class post office. By the time of his retirement, the post office was approaching the status of being a grade ten first-class post office.[87] From a newspaper discussing his retirement in 1965, Alvah told the paper that he:

> Looks forward to cooking Brunswick stew and rock muddle for gatherings of his friends. He hopes to do some fishing, take long trips with his wife and prepare income tax returns as he has done for many years.[88]

On July 18, 1975, Alvah Early passed away at the age of eighty. After his death, a resolution was read and unanimously adopted by the members of the Sixth Judicial District Bar at their annual meeting in Roanoke Rapids, North Carolina, on November 14, 1975, which was sent to Josephine, along with a short note of sympathy regarding Alvah Early's passing. The resolution gave an overview of Alvah's life and spoke of him in high esteem.[89]

Josephine lived eleven more years, passing away at age eighty-nine. Alvah and Josephine had only one child, Emily, my grandmother. Emily Rose Early was born on April 1, 1921, in Norfolk, Virginia. She grew up in Ahoskie, Hertford County, North Carolina. Emily grew up on North Street, Ahoskie, North Carolina. Her future husband, Jesse Watson Barnes, grew up on First Street, only a block away from her. Emily attended the Woman's College of the University of North Carolina in Greensboro, later earning her Bachelor of Arts on June 8, 1942. Emily later married Lieutenant Jesse Watson Barnes on December 5, 1942, just days before Jesse was to be shipped off with the rest of his unit to fight in World War II. Jesse was twenty-one and Emily the same age. After the war, Emily continued to live in Ahoskie with her family. Eventually, Jesse passed away on March 29, 2002, at the age of eighty-one, leaving Emily a widow. Emily lived for two more years, passing away on June 13, 2004, at the age of eighty-three.[90]

Emily and Jesse had three children, the youngest of whom is my mother, Martha Early Barnes, born June 7, 1955, in Ahoskie, Hertford County, North Carolina. Martha was the only girl born to Emily and Jesse, and attended Ahoskie Grade school before going to the Peace College in Raleigh, North Carolina. She then subsequently transferred to East Carolina University in Greenville, North Carolina. She graduated in December 1977 with a degree in Special Education. On October 18, 1980, Martha married her first husband, Clifford Stanley Strickland Jr. Martha was twenty-five, and Clifford also the same age. Their marriage lasted for three years until the couple divorced on July 11, 1983. On September 9, 1983, Martha married Arthur Harris. The couple had two boys, Jesse Quentin Harris, and Timothy Davis Harris. They separated in 2005 and eventually divorced in 2007. In 2010, Martha and her sons relocated to Bluffton, South Carolina, where she is currently a teacher in Beaufort, South Carolina.[91]

The Name of Barnes

The surname Barnes has several possible origins. A very standard origin is that Barnes is the occupational name given to someone who worked at a barn or lived by one. The habitational origin is the Old English name for the location on the Surrey bank of the Thames in London, which was Barnes. Another possible origin is from the name of someone born by the son or servant of a barne, a word that is derived from the Old English "beorn" and the Old Norse barn, meaning "young warrior." A possible Irish origin is the Gaelic Ó Bearáin, or, "descendant of Bearán." The surname Barnes had at least nineteen coat of arms. The reoccurring elements include the colors azure (blue), yellow or gold, argent (white or silver), sable (black), and gules (red).[92] The shield also contained either lions, leopards, or a cross or sets of crosses.[93] Leopards were said to represent 'a valiant and hardy warrior, who enterprises hazardous things by force and courage.' The crosses have multitudes of styles and meanings, and unless the history is known, there is no telling what one might mean by itself, other than a possible reference to Christ or Christianity.[94]

The Barnes Family

The Barnes line of my family begins with James B. Barnes, born in Virginia around 1803. It is unclear when James moved to North Carolina, but on December 15, 1823, James married Salley Ramsay in Northampton County, North Carolina. It is peculiar to note that multiple records of this marriage exist, along with different dates, some also have different years. Currently, it is unclear why this would be, other than there being multiple people with the same name. The entire Barnes family does not appear until the 1850 Federal Census, which places them in Northampton County, North Carolina. The property that they owned was valued at $3,200. James' wife is listed as "Sarah S Barnes," and upon further investigation, I discovered that "Salley" or "Sallie" was often a nickname for Sarah.[95] There is an 1860 Slave Census Schedule with the name "Jas B Barnes" on it, "Jas" being the abbreviation of James, with the location of Northampton, North Carolina. Still, other than that, there is no way to confirm that this is the same James Barnes in my line of descent. There is also the 1860 U.S. Census that lists the Barnes household, though unlike the 1850 U.S.

Census, lists most of the household as being from Virginia, instead of only James Barnes. After the 1860 Census, all records for James Barnes stop, other than his name being on the death certificates of his children. There is information that points to James B Barnes and his youngest son, James B Barnes Jr, having fought and died in the Civil War on the Confederate side. Because this information was only available at the National Archives in Washington, D.C., or behind a paywall, I can neither confirm nor deny that James fought in the Civil War. Assuming James B. Barnes Sr. died in the Civil War, he would have been around sixty years old. Sarah appears in the 1870 U.S. Census, but it does not say whether she is married, which would indicate if James was still alive, or if she is widowed, which would confirm James's death. The reason this may not be Sarah is that her name is listed as Sallie, and she is listed as living in Wilson, North Carolina, not Northampton. Sarah appears again in the 1880 U.S. Census in Northampton County, living with her daughter and son in-law. After this census, all records for Sarah stop. There is a death index for a Sarah Barnes passing away from cancer in Wilson, but the date listed is August 1879, so it is unlikely this is the same person. Assuming that Sarah passed away in 1880, she would have been seventy-two years old.[96]

It is unclear how many children James and Sarah had, but the 1850 U.S. Census shows at least six children. Out of those six children, the line continues next with Richard Barnes. There is no exact birthday for Richard, but the 1850 U.S. Census puts him as being born sometime around

1828. The 1850 census lists Richard, at nineteen years old, as being a student. On December 11, 1856, in Bertie County, North Carolina, Richard Barnes married Elizabeth Veale. Richard was twenty-eight and Elizabeth eighteen years old. Unlike his father and brothers, I was able to confirm that Richard fought in the Civil War. He is recorded as having enlisted on August 9, 1862, at thirty-three years of age. The difference in age between the roster and the 1850 U.S. Census is barely a year, so it is highly likely this is the same Richard Barnes in my ancestry. Richard was enlisted in Company F of the North Carolina 4th Cavalry Regiment on September 1, 1862. He is listed as having survived the war, and only the rank of Private is shown. After the war, Richard continued living in Bertie County, North Carolina, for at least the next fifteen years as a farmer, this being listed in both the 1870 and 1880 censuses. Richard died before 1900, somewhere between age fifty-two and seventy-three. Elizabeth appears as widowed in the 1900 U.S. Census and lived with her daughter, Fannie, and Fannie's husband. After the 1900 Census, records stop for Elizabeth. It can be assumed that she died sometime between 1901 and 1910, between sixty-two and seventy-two years old.[97]

According to the 1900 U.S. Census, Richard and Elizabeth had a total of nine children. Out of those nine children, my ancestry continues through William James Barnes. William was born on September 12, 1859, in North Carolina. William grew up in Bertie County, North Carolina, eventually going to work on his father's farm at the age of twenty, as recorded by the 1880 Federal

Census. Sometime between 1880 and 1900, William married Rosa Lee Parker. Both are recorded together with their children in the 1900 U.S. Census, William thirty-nine and Rosa forty years old years old. Sometime between 1900 and 1903, at the latest, Rosa passed away, though the reason why is unknown. Between 1900 and 1903, William met and married a widow who had three children from a previous marriage, Sallie, Jessie, and Cherry Bazemore.[98] Sallie would have been around thirty-one years old at the time. William worked as a farmer in North Carolina until sometime between 1920 and 1930 when he shows up in the 1930 U.S. Census for Norfolk, Virginia. On September 18, 1937, William James Barnes passed away at the age of seventy-eight in Norfolk, Virginia. Sallie lived one year longer than William, passing away on April 19, 1940, at the age of seventy-one.[99]

William, Rosa, and Sallie had a combined total of fifteen children. My line of descent continues through William and Rosa from their third child, John Bailey Barnes, Sr. John Bailey Barnes Sr. was born August 21, 1885, in Bertie County, North Carolina. He attended grade school in Woodville, North Carolina. By 1910, John worked in the travel industry doing commercial work, living in Roxobel, North Carolina. On September 5, 1917, John Bailey Barnes married Jessie Eunice Watson, who was born in Northampton County, North Carolina.[100] Jessie was a distant relative through her mother's side to the Barnes family. Jessie's mother was Martha Sarah Woodard Watson, and Martha's mother was Anna Maria Barnes Woodard, the daughter of James B

Barnes and Sarah Ramsay. When John Bailey and Jessie were married, John was thirty-two years old, and Jessie, nineteen. Between 1917 and 1918, John Bailey registered for the draft for World War I and helped operate the Barnes Brothers retail firm. On September 1, 1919, John Bailey and J. L. Sawyer, opened Barnes-Sawyer Wholesale Grocery in Ahoskie.[101] By 1920, the Barnes family had settled in Ahoskie, North Carolina. In 1946, the Barnes-Sawyer building caught fire and burned down, the estimated damage totaling up to a loss of $250,000. The building was rebuilt afterward. On August 15, 1950, John Bailey Barnes Sr. passed away at age sixty-four. Jessie Eunice Watson lived for thirty-one more years, passing away on June 27, 1981, in Pitt County, North Carolina, at age eighty-three.[102]

John Bailey Barnes Sr. and Jessie Eunice Watson had three children, the line of descent continuing through Jesse (Jack) Watson Barnes, who was born February 17, 1921, in Ahoskie, Hertford County, North Carolina. Jesse grew up on First Street in Ahoskie, only a block away from his future wife, Emily Rose Early, who lived on North Street. Eventually, Jesse, who went by, Jack. He attended the University of North Carolina in Chapel Hill, joining the Alpha Tau Chapter of the Sigma Chi Fraternity, on April 13, 1940. The Chapter is "dedicated to three primary principles: friendship, justice, and learning." Jack traveled to Montgomery, Alabama, and on September 4, 1941, enlisted in the Air Corps as an Aviation Cadet. Jack was fresh out of school, graduating from the University of North Carolina, where he completed a Bachelor of Science degree in commerce. As a flight student, Jack was at the Air Force Base in Coleman, Texas, at the time of the bombing of Pearl Harbor.[103]

Building In Ahoskie Burns At Loss of $250,000

Firemen in the above picture are shown fighting the worst fire in the history of Ahoskie. The fire destroyed Hertford County's largest brick building, a three-story wholesale grocery warehouse, early Friday morning. J. Bailey Barnes of Ahoskie, a proprietor of the Barnes-Sawyer Grocery Company, estimated the loss of foodstuff and household goods at $200,000. W. H. Basnight of Ahoskie, owner of the building, estimated his loss at $50,000.

Figure 2.2: Newspaper coverage on the Barnes-Sawyer that burned down in 1946. Newspaper clipping in the personal collection of the author.

On February 26, 1942, Jack completed his basic flight training at Randolph Field, Texas, and was then ready to move on to advanced training. He was commissioned as a second lieutenant and was soon put on active duty. On December 5, 1942, Jack and Emily were married, both twenty-one years old. Days later, Jack was sent off to the war front, participating in missions such as anti-submarine patrol flights in Northwest Africa. During the war, Jack flew a Consolidated B-24 Liberator. The B-24 was a crucial bomber in the Allied Forces strategy during World War II.[104] Not only was it the most produced American aircraft of the entire war, but it also proved essential to combating U-boats. Liberators were crewed by seven to ten personnel: the pilot, the co-pilot, the navigator, the nose gunner, the bombardier, the dorsal turret gunner, and the radioman.[105] Flights in this theater of war eventually earned Jack an Air Medal with a bronze Oak Leaf Cluster for meritorious achievement.[106]

Jack survived the war, returning home sometime in 1945, and began starting a family with Emily. Around 1959, Jack was working as the treasurer for Barnes-Sawyer Wholesale Grocery Company. Later in life, Jack rekindled his dream of being a Certified Public Accountant (CPA). He worked under a CPA and opened his own accounting office in Ahoskie. From the same article that spoke of Jack's memories of World War II:

> Meanwhile his bookkeeping and tax service offices are at 112 N. Mitchell. Yes, he still carries a pilot's license in his pocket. Only he hasn't kept up his physicals, he says with a sheepish smile, the big deterrent to active flying. "Get the CPA first, and then maybe..." He looks up with a faraway expression.[107]

Despite passing the test knowledge-wise, Jack was unable to pass the CPA certification in the limited time for the exam. To him and his closest family members, it was heartbreaking.

J. W. Barnes Nears CPA Dreams

AHOSKIE — The laughter lines and the tiny crows feet etched by squinting to look into the sun streaming through into his tightly cramped cockpit are a little deeper than they were. So are the worry lines in his forehead.

His hair is a great deal sparser.

But his memories of those days as a B-24 pilot over the Atlantic and the Mediterranean are as vivid as though he hunted submarines yesterday instead of over two decades back.

J. W. (Jack) Barnes is a father now of three, the eldest 19 and old enough to pilot bombers himself if he were so minded. But the boy's going to be an engineer Barnes will tell you.

Then divert the conversation to piloting and Barnes' World War II experiences, and his memories are flowing as rapidly as a river, and his eyes light up with nostalgia.

It's a long time ago now, but those sub-patrol days were exciting. So long as they could keep the subs in sight they couldn't surface to recharge their batteries — atomic subs were then many years in the future.

There were those off-shore patrols from Africa, when the bomber pilots knew "something big" was coming off but hadn't any ideas.

It was their job to be on submarine guard and they were as the big troop ships moved beneath them.

It also was their job to be alert in case a maraudering enemy fighter plane came in from out of the sun.

They were shot at more than once — and once was by a submarine from about 50 feet below the bomber's wings as they flew above the water. But the

JESSE W. (Jack) BARNES

Figure 2.3: Newspaper coverage of Jesse (Jack) Watson Barnes, "World War II Interrupted But J. W. Barnes Nears CPA Dreams," *The Herald*, n.d. Clipping in the personal collection of the author.

On March 29, 2002, after a week of being in the hospital, Jack passed away. Emily lived for two more years, passing away on June 16, 2004. Their oldest, John Davis Barnes, lives in Greensboro, North Carolina, with his wife, Helen Sparrow Barnes. Their second child, Timothy Woodard Barnes, lives in Savannah, Georgia, with his wife Mary Ann Doughtie Barnes, near their daughter Allison Early Barnes and her daughter. Their youngest and only daughter, Martha Early Barnes, lives in Bluffton, South Carolina.[108]

The Future of My Preservation

"What is *your* heritage and the state of its preservation?" is the question I have been attempting to answer. Currently, I feel that I still do not have an answer. Admittedly, I have a significant amount of historical data that I have collected. I am now able to trace my family further back than I would have thought possible. At the same time, I feel like I still know very little about the people I have been researching. In my research, I came across an article containing an excerpt from author Joseph Amato's novel *Jacob's Well: A Case for Rethinking Family History*. Amato discussed how family history is not just history, but the combination of history and storytelling.[109] This hit close to what I have felt that I am missing from the information I currently have. Take, for instance, Thompson Harris III and his siblings, Hampton and Frances. Records show that these members of the Harris family moved from North Carolina to Georgia. *Pioneers of Wiregrass Georgia* says that the Harris family moved to Georgia sometime around 1800. However, the account given in *Pioneers of Wiregrass Georgia* is suspect as the information within has been proven to be inaccurate.

So, it is unclear when they actually moved to Georgia, if anyone besides the three siblings accompanied them, and most importantly, why they made this move. There is little information available from between the 1790 census and the 1850 census.[110] Until more information comes to light, it will remain a mystery. The same goes for the Early family. There is possible evidence that James Early was born in Ireland, then sentenced to one of the prison colonies in Australia. This James Early served his prison sentence and then made his way to America. Because of a lack of documents, I cannot confirm that this is the James Early in my family tree. On top of this, his wife is only known by her first name, Priscila. All four branches of my family can only be traced to early America. This is not insignificant, but it makes me eager to see if I can find out the answer.

Another question that remains unanswered for now is, how did the members of my family tree grow and change during the nineteenth century. I can only confirm that two ancestors were involved in the Civil War, fighting on the Confederate side. Besides knowing that these two members fought in the war, I know nothing about their thoughts and feelings on what they were fighting for or what their experiences were. The fact that they were fighting on the side of the Confederates suggests to me that they were fighting to uphold slavery. There are slave index records that have names that match those of my ancestors as slave owners. Although it would be convenient to ignore data that would confirm that my ancestors were slave owners, it would not be the truth. With the rise in popularity of genealogy, picking and choosing what facts to acknowledge has become an unfortunate but popular choice.[111] Aaron Sheehan-Dean discusses the effort to focus on the effects that the Civil War had on America up to today. He discusses the earlier historians saw the Civil War as something that unified America, but now the focus has shifted to the numerous impacts the Civil War had.[112] My ancestors all lived in the American South during the nineteenth century. Sheehan-Dean paraphrases another history professor, Peter Carmichael, and his argument that in the years after the Civil War, many white southerners who came of age in the 1850s remained committed to "traditional" southern values even after taking the loyalty oath. Sheehan-Dean quotes Carmichael, who argued that the young white southerners of the post-war period "remained committed to a new Americanism based on romantic sentimentalism, scientific racism, laissez-fair economics, and imperialism."[113] I do not know if my ancestors identified as these type of southerners, or if they fought for another reason.

The herstory of the women in my family tree is also lacking. This can be attributed to a belief and treatment of women that only assumes their role as wives and housemakers.[114] This then makes women merely additions to the household, as if they were objects rather than people.[115] I even found myself contributing to this in my research, focusing more on the male members in my paternal and maternal lines. Few oral stories have been passed down through my family. Until I can find more information, my heritage will be incomplete. But then again, perhaps the process of research is what is the most important, and not the final destination, because there is always more to learn.

There are two areas of my family history that I am especially interested in discovering more about. The first is Thompson Harris III and his son George. While I would love to be able to find more information about Thompson and his origins, what most intrigues me is that he and his son both did blacksmith work. During the nineteenth century, blacksmiths went from being the ideal representation of individual strength and industry to being replaced by machines, making blacksmiths obsolete. [116] Before the Industrial Revolution, blacksmiths were fundamental to communities. [117] What then did Thompson and George contribute to their communities, and does anything made by them survive? I do not know the answer.

The second area of interest I came across by happenstance. When looking into the background of the Capps and Harris families, I discovered that Kannapolis, the area where Arthur Clarence and Susie Louise moved to, was not an ordinary town, but the largest mill village in America. [118] Like many mill communities in North Carolina, Kannapolis practiced paternalism or, as defined by the Oxford Dictionary, the policy or practice on the part of people in positions of authority of restricting the freedom and responsibilities of those subordinate to them in the subordinates' supposed best interest.' [119] Arthur Clarence Harris and Susie Louise Conner worked for Cannon Mills between 1940 and 1946. [120] The owner, Charles Cannon, controlled the Kannapolis's economic, political, and social climate and so vehemently resisted unionization. He owned almost every street, home, and store. Cannon was so involved with the lives of his workers that the workers themselves were an extension of him. The employees felt they owed him everything. According to union organizers attempting to infiltrate Cannon Mills, the employees were even isolated, working behind fences. The town had no hotels or rental properties.[121] Cannon was still alive when Arthur and Susie worked at Cannon Mills, and the environment was still the same. This is shocking to me. I know nothing about what went on with my family members there, and it is something I wish to know more about. I also believe that in a broader sense that people no longer see history as relevant. If we fail to know where we started, then I believe we cannot progress forward because we have no way of orienting where we want to go. Preserving the past, especially our own, is one of the most important actions we can take.

Chapter 3: Stewards of the Blue Ridge Foothills

By Jackson Royall

Prologue

Sunrise always seems to take hours while in the woods, waiting. There are no lights, save for the stars and moon; my senses are heightened as I walk, listening over the crunching leaves underfoot and the crisp Carolina winter wind that chills my exposed face. My limbs are heavy, layered with thick clothing to protect me from the cold. My hands gingerly grip my .308 caliber hunting rifle. The world seems as though it is still asleep; however, I feel that every hidden eye in the forest is observing me. Soon, though, I find my place among the wild, where I will sit and watch, patiently, for movement in the darkness. A dim glow fills the air as the sun slowly begins to illuminate the earth around me, though it is far from light. Shadows move about in the field. I do not trust my eyes in the darkness; I use my peripheral vision to discern if the shadows are alive, or if they are mere illusions in my mind. A thin streak of orange separates the horizon from the sky, and the world around me begins to breathe with life. Across the field, I recognize the familiar silhouette of an old homestead, reclaimed by the wilderness long ago. I know my father sits somewhere near it, and I feel at peace knowing I am not alone.

In the growing light, grey foxes scurry out of their burrows to feed. Limbs of pine and maple trees, bare in the wintertime, dance in the breeze –

the crowns of the trees bathing in the luminescent red-orange glow of the sunrise. The shadows I was skeptical of in the darkness are clear figures now, frolicking in the field and scanning the ground for food while their ears constantly flutter with alertness. The coming light has revealed the identity of the shadows – three whitetail deer, a large doe and two fawns. I make no move for my rifle. Instead, I watch them with a close curiosity and a great deal of respect. They move gingerly, with care in each step; they scan their surroundings thoroughly before taking another, repeating this process as they move about the field. Soon more join the original three, and they begin to move with more freedom, confident in their numbers. Suddenly, though, they stop, heads high and alert, tails flickering like a white flag in the wind. They stare intently in my direction, standing so still they could be lifeless; I fear they have scented me, or have somehow heard a sound that I did not make. Regardless, I match their stature and do not dare to move. In my peripheral vision, I catch movement to my right. I begin slowly turning my head to look directly towards it, though I have already noticed its barrel-like torso, broad shoulders and neck, and antlers branching far outwards.

The deer in the field did not notice me; they noticed the audacious buck, striding slowly out to meet them. Rut has made him careless, unconcerned about anything but a mate. My heartbeat rises in my ears over the silence of dawn as I raise my rifle to my cheek; my breath becomes rapid and shallow with the anxious adrenaline all hunters know. I follow him with my scope for mere moments, waiting what seems like centuries for him to turn broadside. Finally, he stops. As my adrenaline rises, I exhale, attempting to steady the crosshair just behind his shoulder. At the bottom of my exhale, my heart pounds like a drum in my ears. Focused, I gently squeeze the trigger. My rifle erupts into my shoulder as the tranquility of the early morning turns to chaos for a moment in time. The smoke clears, and I begin to scan the field…

Introduction

The Royall family has been traced back to 1086 C.E., where two instances of Royalls appear in the *Domesday Book* commissioned by the Norman-born English king, William the Conqueror, following his conquest of England twenty years earlier. The generations of Royalls that follow, from England to America, have been well documented; records such as court acquittals, guild member information, and property deeds dating to fourteenth century Essex, England have been gathered to the best abilities of my family members prior research. In fact, there is such an abundance of information available, it was challenging to pinpoint where to begin my own story. While all of the Royall names and the places they come from have led me to where I am today, I do not feel that they all have shaped what I define as my own heritage. Thus, instead of outwardly seeking what questions to ask in regard to what my heritage may be through research and observations, I looked inward – how has the past shaped my heritage, my sense of place, and what I take pride in? What do I share with both my immediate family and my ancestors, and what can I preserve for future generations?

In my earliest memories, I recall spending my time outdoors with family. As a seventh generation Floridian on my mother's side, I grew up hunting, camping, and exploring freely in the humid oak hammocks, palmetto scrub, and prairies of central and north Florida. I do not remember my first time holding or shooting a rifle – my father ensured that it become second nature at a young age. My father was a housing developer for Palmer Ranch during the late-2000s recession; the land between I-75 and Myakka State Park that was intended to be for houses was left in its natural state, for a time, due to the blunders of human economics. We had private access to thousands of acres, untouched by humans save for dirt roads, a handful of early twentieth century cattle-cracker shacks, and old cow pens. Cattle grazed, wild creatures ran unabated, and the stars shined bright in the night sky. Each morning, I would emerge from my tent reluctantly; the coolness of the morning made leaving my sleeping bag difficult. However, the early morning dew, dense fog over the field, and the cool dawn air were not enough to deter me from the scent of breakfast cooking in a cast iron over an open fire, just a short walk down the dirt path from the field into the oaks and palmetto scrub. Among the oak hammock was an aging homestead consisting of a wooden vernacular Florida cracker shack and a metal outbuilding, abandoned sometime in the mid-twentieth century. We made camp here habitually; over time, we installed a water pump, built a large doghouse for our chocolate Labrador

Retriever, Riley, and lit fires in the same spot so many times there was a permanent pit. Wild citrus trees grew by the old houses – bitter to the taste, though refreshing in the Florida heat.

Every passing day brought the same activities that were somehow different each time. After breakfast, we would load up in the bed of a pickup truck or onto our all-terrain vehicles (ATVs) and ride with no particular destination in mind. The activity was typically the same, but the experience varied. Some days were quiet rides through cow pasture. Others, we encounter large packs of wild pigs, or spooked a herd of deer. Some days, flocks of birds so dense they cast a shadow flew overhead. By noon, the Florida sun bore down too hot, and forced us back into the shade until the evening. We would often spend our afternoons in the field where we pitched our tents, shooting clay skeets with our shotguns from the shade provided by ancient oak trees ornamented with Spanish moss. Friends of my parents often came. When I was young, I would lead their children around and find something to get into that we shouldn't be near, antagonizing yellowjackets with rocks or prodding a diamondback rattlesnake until it gave us its musical warning. We would wait eagerly for nightfall so we could play manhunt in the field, searching and hiding for what felt like hours, running through the tall reeds and sawgrass of the nearby bog with bliss.

As often as we could, we would spend our time camping in the wilderness. We hunted feral hogs, Osceola turkey, and whitetail deer; fished in lakes and streams. We had what seemed like all the time in the world at our fingertips. We interacted with Florida in a way most people won't ever know. Through it all, we built trust and confidence with one another, as well as a deeper connection to our natural surroundings. These are among my most cherished memories, and I often find that when my mind wanders, it is back to these Floridian places sacred to my youth. The time I spent in the wild during my youth began my journey down the path of understanding my own historical lineage.

Local Landscape

My father comes from a multi-generational legacy of homesteading hunters and trappers of the foothills of the Blue Ridge Mountains in western North Carolina. Each year at Thanksgiving we make the ten-hour trek there to spend a week with our family, and to hunt whitetail deer. I have spent countless hours with my father, grandfather, uncle, and cousin, all born of the area, either preparing for the season or seeking an ever-elusive buck. What once was part of an age-old livelihood for our family has become our tradition that we honor each year. Historically, the Royalls in America have depended upon their connection to natural surroundings for survival. Although we do not depend on hunting for sustenance today, we preserve the memories and cultural heritage of the Royall family through its pursuit; my ancestors' connection to their natural surroundings was a crucial aspect of their well-being. Their structures, tangible material culture, oral histories, memories and transferrable knowledge cultivated from generations of hunting and living with a connection to the outdoors are evidence of the relationship they had with their natural surroundings. This relationship is reflected within their social and community environments, and their socioeconomic status as the rural South transitioned from the Old to the New. Through modern hunting, we practice land conservation in hopes that we may be able to pass our traditions on to those who come after us, and we preserve a livelihood slowly being lost.

Near the intersection of Highway 421 and I-77 in western North Carolina lies the small, unincorporated community of Hamptonville, Yadkin County. The community, set aside by Revolutionary War Colonel, Henry Hampton in 1807 and chartered in 1818, is situated over an hour's drive north of Charlotte, and nearly an hour west of Winston-Salem.[1] Those passing by on the highway likely pay it no mind, other than as a place to fill up their gas tank. From the highway, only a few gas stations and run-down motels, a flea market, and a local diner called Debbie's Snack Bar are visible among dense pine trees. On any given autumn morning, the Snack Bar's gravel parking lot is full – men dressed in woodland camouflage coats, overalls, and hunter-orange hats visit habitually for coffee and breakfast. Turning off the highway, southbound down old Highway 21, one passes a wooden roadside sign reading "Welcome to Hamptonville" in capital white letters. The two-lane highway winds through rolling hills, dense pine forests, timber-lined ridges, through deep hollows, over small branches and flowing rivers. The Hamptonville landscape is characterized by farmhouses set far back from the road, rolling fields of corn and soy, along with remains of aged homesteads of a time long past, reclaimed by wilderness and veiled in mystery. In the winter, when the trees are bare, one can see Pilot Mountain rising over the hills to the east, and the hazy Blue Ridge Mountains in the west. The valley that lies between is the same land my ancestors roamed and hunted since the 1800s.

Prior to the construction and completion of the American interstate systems, those travelling by road often took Highway 21 from Cleveland, Ohio to Yamasee, South Carolina. It was one of few routes that connected the South to the North through the Blue Ridge and Appalachian ranges, and was a main artery from the Great Lakes to the coastal South.[2] As such, it was a significant socioeconomic resource for towns built upon it. Interstate systems along with suburbanization and the rise of automobile use drastically changed cultural and historic landscapes in rural areas. Thousands of acres were cleared for interstate construction, altering natural landscapes and demolishing historic structures. Existing roadways were often replaced or re-routed to better suit the interstate systems being constructed. Old highways were general access roads that allowed a direct interaction between travelers and the streetscapes of communities. Lined by businesses with direct frontal access in rural main street settings, these roads were traveled at slower speeds, and were characterized by distinct vernacular architecture that offered travelers a direct link to the local landscape, as well as the community itself. [3]

The pattern in which travelers interacted with rural communities changed upon the completion of interstate systems, reconfiguring the built environment of American towns. Vernacular architectural styles became obscure along with their formerly lively communities.[4] Local, family owned businesses built with direct access to old highways struggled to scrape by as high-speed travelers now came and went with little to no interaction, as if they were never truly there at all. Those living in rural settings now had almost no choice but to commute via interstate to larger commercial centers for employment, diminishing the workforce within rural communities.[5] Local businesses cannot afford to compete at modern interstate interchanges; instead, they are often occupied by gas stations, name-brand restaurant chains, big-box stores, and strip shopping malls.[6] Cultural and architectural uniqueness is lost to the same colorless landscape one might see at a typical interstate exit. The intimate details of local landscapes become a blur as travelers race to their destination along a route pre-determined by an app on their mobile device.

Hamptonville is no exception to the plights rural communities face in lieu of interstate construction. Hamptonville did not have a singular main street; instead, its local commercial centers were characterized by a handful of family owned restaurants or general stores built at intersections of country roads. As a child in the mid-1970s, my father recalls riding his bicycle up to Woods General Store for a "grape soda and a bologna sandwich" regularly.[7] It was small, intimate interactions with local communities that kept family operated commerce alive. At some point, the general store burned down; there was no incentive to rebuild, and the crossroads of Highway 21 and Hamptonville Road where it once stood is now empty. These once-vibrant commercial intersections share similar fates. Historic buildings of vernacular styles that were formerly family owned businesses remain vacant and often in disrepair.

Rural Life in Hamptonville

It is here, within the Hamptonville community and the surrounding countryside, where my father was born and raised. He was born in 1968 to Hubert "Bud" Royall, a life-long forklift driver for Joseph Schlitz Brewing, and Vivian Royall, a hairdresser. His older brother Jeffrey, who passed away in 2017, was born in 1966, and his sister Cary was born in 1978. They were raised in a small, single-story mid-century brick house that Bud built in 1954 on the bank of a small creek, overlooking distant rolling hills and timbered ridgelines along a winding country road. Hunting, river fishing, and trapping were as commonplace as any other activity among the community, and were pastimes that the family shared together. He recalls squirrel and rabbit hunting with his father, grandfather, and brother in the hills around their home. They often trapped turtles for stew, and would fish in the Yadkin River for flathead and channel catfish, along with largemouth bass. My father remembers being chased by wild dogs by the river, encountering packs of coyotes, families of bears, and a few close encounters with copperhead rattlesnakes. He and his siblings played in the forests and hills where their forefathers lived, often at the old log-hewn homestead that his grandfather built and where his father was raised.

My father earned wages off of odd jobs during his formative years. Picking tobacco, working with livestock and in large chicken coops were typical opportunities for employment available to boys in their youth. He graduated from Starmount High School in 1986, and attended Carson-Newman University in Jefferson, Tennessee on a wrestling scholarship. He was the first in his family to attend and graduate from college, and was among the first generation within the family to complete high school. He met my mother while at Carson-Newman, and following her graduation in 1994, they moved back to her hometown of Bradenton, Florida. It was here that I was born and raised, a generation removed from the Blue Ridge foothills. As such, I have a unique perspective of the area that has assisted in my analysis for thesis research. Our yearly Thanksgiving family trips, along with other summer or winter break excursions to both hunt and visit, have allotted me enough time there to show me what life is like with insight to the lives of my father, grandfather, and the rest of my family still living there without experiencing the potential drawbacks. Poor employment opportunities, education, and healthcare have always been issues that the community has faced. Hardships such as cyclical debt can drive individuals to abuse alcohol or prescription drugs, and even suicide. Living in a naturally beautiful place comes at a cost, and many fall victim to the vices and unseen traps that are set behind the veil. My father believes that deciding to follow the path elsewhere, out of the community, was one of the best decisions he has made; those who stay often struggle to find success and succumb to the hardships rural life can bring.

A life of hardship and borderline poverty has been a recurring theme for the Royall family in North Carolina for generations. My grandfather Hubert Royall, who I refer to as "Papaw", was born in a wooden cabin in 1942, built by his father Hubert Jennings Royall, or "Papaw Hubert" as I knew him, sometime in the 1930s in Hamptonville. Papaw recalls looking outside "through gaps between wooden walls" while lying in his bed to sleep, and could feel the cold seeping through the cracks during the winter months. [8] They used newspaper for insulation during the winter, and supported parts of the metal roof with bare pine limbs. The house was built using hand cut and hand hewn pine; a fading method of construction by the 1930s, as mills had become commonplace. The structure is a story high, with crawlspace in the attic, now filled with cobwebs and other un-pleasantries. Stepping up onto the elevated porch, one must be cautions of disturbing copperhead rattlesnakes that enjoy the shade provided underneath. Wild grass and weeds grow high around the structure during the spring and summer, and vines reach high upon its wooden walls. Though it has remained empty since the 1950s, it has endured heavy rains and snowfalls, along with high winds from hurricanes for a decade shy of a century. My great-grandfather Papaw Hubert, born in 1917, built the homestead nestled down in a hollow among tall loblolly pine trees, roughly twenty yards from a mountain spring.

Figure 3.1: Papaw retracing his footsteps at his old home. Photograph by the author.

The original windows of the house remain intact, though are weathered with age. Remains of other past structures rest nearby; a collapsed barn lies across a small stream, along with the remains of a stone foundation and chimney that stand a short walk away. For a time, it was among the final self-sustaining homesteads of the Appalachian Mountains; water could be drawn from the spring, food such as corn and potatoes were grown by the nearby stream, and a meager amount of livestock was kept at the now-collapsed barn. Papaw Hubert would leave before sun-up to hunt for rabbit, squirrels, turkey or deer, while my great-grandmother Mamaw Lucille would prepare a Southern breakfast of sausage, grits, gravy, and ho cakes on cast-iron skillets and a Dutch oven. As a child, my grandfather would chop logs for the furnace and retrieve pails of water from the spring daily. During planting seasons, he would assist his father in plowing the field and planting the crop, and during harvesting seasons he would assist in gathering, preserving, and storing what they grew. For a time, my great-grandfather made a living off of hunting and trapping; what meats or furs he did not use himself or in contribution to homestead life, he sold to local markets.

Eventually, Papaw Hubert and family could no longer sustain the lifestyle the Royall's had known since they arrived in the American South. My grandfather recalls the prices for the things they needed to buy from town growing too high, while large plots of land were being bought up and used to grow tobacco, the nation's emerging cash-crop. The family could no longer be sustained by hunting, trapping, homesteading, or performing other occasional odd jobs. In the late 1940s, my great-grandfather began working for various local textile mills and then the Schlitz Brewing factory. This ended homesteading for the Royall family, as industrialization had finally caught up to them.

While the property on which the homestead was built is no longer owned by my family, the tract is only good for timber and will never be developed. Further, it is leased by Backwoods Hunt Club, a subsidiary of Backwoods Outdoors, Incorporated, which was established by my father, Mark Royall, my late uncle Jeff, and Papaw. Originally managed by Jeff, it is now under ownership and management by my cousin, Channing Royall, with assistance from my father and other club members. At times, the house has been used as a hunting lodge of sorts; it is by no means luxurious, and is somewhat creepy. However, it offers shelter and ease of access to the surrounding landscape when hunting at sunrise. Hunting from the old house offers some perspective as to what it was truly like living in the house when my grandfather and great-grandfather did. On a cold morning, before sunrise, one emerges from a bundle of blankets in a sleeping bag to the smell of coffee boiling over an open flame in the old hearth, as there is no electricity. The house is bitter cold – opening the door to the wilderness brings a frigid chill that sweeps inside. However, stepping quietly off the wooden porch onto the grass, one is soon immersed in the wild, just as my grandfather and great-grandfather had done so many mornings.

Backwoods Hunting Club

Since its 2008 inception in Hamptonville, North Carolina, Backwoods Hunt Club has acquired over 8,500 acres in Iredell, Davie, Surry, Alleghany, Caldwell, Wilkes, and Yadkin counties in North Carolina and also Patrick County, Virginia.[9] Other than hunting, the Club's foremost goal is to ensure responsibility and stewardship over Club properties with principles derived from Quality Deer Management standards to legally ensure ethical practices. All Club members take part in wildlife management and land conservation to both improve the hunting experience and to preserve it for future use. Club land includes corn and soy farmland, softwood timber and rugged hardwood tracts, as well as mountainous tracts within the Blue Ridge mountain range. Over the years, the Club has allowed us to hunt different areas and landscapes throughout northwestern North Carolina and southern Virginia – the same lands that my ancestors have been traversing since the late eighteenth century, from the Yadkin River Valley to the Blue Ridge Mountains.

As the son of a Club founder, I have had the opportunity to see firsthand the amount of time, effort, and love for the wild that goes into keeping these properties fit for hunting. We have spent countless hours as a family exploring tracts around North Carolina and Virginia, preparing deer stands, planting food plots, and building deer feeders – all while traversing mountains and thick forests. The overarching purpose is to hunt whitetail deer; however, if we did not spend our time in the wild with one another, it would not feel worthwhile. At times, there is little work to be done; we still opt to spend our time riding and walking the lands we hunt. We familiarize ourselves with the sights and sounds of the landscape – we listen to the wind rustling through the leaves, noting its direction. We scan the forest for signs of deer – watching for tracks in the dirt, scrapes on tree trunks where bucks have marked their territory with their antlers, and gaps through thickets where wildlife have worn in their own path. Unknowingly, each step we take and each time we stop to listen we pay a little homage to our forefathers. Today, we hunt, fish, and occasionally trap with the intention of making a meal, and with the genuine enjoyment of the pastime. We no longer pursue it as a necessity as our forefathers once did. To them, hunting was not so much a choice as it was a means of survival; both monetarily, through the furs or whatever else they may have sold, as well as how they would feed their families living in isolated homesteads. It was not just something that they did because they had daily access to it, like it often is today. They adhered to it, day in and day out, like a creed.

Preserving Intangible Heritage

Most individuals today, save for those dedicated to living off-grid, cannot or do not need to pursue hunting as a necessity. The requirement of property ownership and the ability to access public or private lands often bars individuals from hunting. Becoming a hunter today is difficult if one is not born or raised with a connection to it; the pastime requires years of mentorship and practice to become skilled. Increasing amounts of people are moving to urban areas, and the amount of land available to hunt is shrinking while also growing more restricted. Further, social trends regarding firearms and the harvest of animals have painted hunters in a negative light. All of these are contributing factors to the decline of participants in the United States, as fewer game licenses are sold each year. According to the U.S. Fish and Wildlife Service, 5 percent of Americans, or 11.5 million people, over the age of 16 actively hunted during 2016 – down from 10 percent, or roughly 20 million people, 50 years ago. The rate of decline is expected to accelerate within the next decade or so.[10]

As responsible hunters, we are conservationists. Adhering to proper harvesting principles ensures that populations of wild game are well-managed within local ecosystems. We respect our lands so that we may continue our outdoor pursuits while protecting our nation's natural resources. The decline in hunters is problematic to ecosystems not only in the sense that there are less stewards of the land; as hunting lands are used at decreasing rates, funding for federal land conservation faces a subsequent decrease. The majority of funding for federal land conservation comes from the sale of hunting licenses, at 35 percent of total funding. Only 15 percent of funding is derived from the Federal Aid in Wildlife Restoration Act, or Pittman-Robertson Act of 1937, which requires states to fund the "selection, restoration, and improvement of wildlife habitat through conservation and research." [11] The remainder comes from miscellaneous sales, taxes, grants, and funds. As these numbers shrink due to the lack of participating hunters, conservation lands face increasing risk of ecosystem mismanagement. Wild game populations, the well-being of ecosystems, and conservation lands as a collective in the modern world face external threats daily as the prospect of economic growth and development bite at their heels. Fish and Wildlife departments around the country manage thousands of plant and animal species alike; without ample funding, the number of endangered plant and animal species could rise from the 1,600 listed today to potentially thousands more.[12]

The future of hunting is uncertain not only in the decreasing number of new participants. Changing climates of the future are inescapable, even for hardy whitetail deer. While their populations are still high, and will remain so, they are undergoing behavioral changes in how they interact with the environment, and which environments they are choosing to live in. Whitetail deer are unique in their ability to rapidly adapt to their environments. Firsthand, I have observed deer change their behavioral patterns over the course of hunting seasons as they encounter and respond to changes in agriculture, weather patterns, and the threat of hunters. If a mature buck so much as catches human scent on the wind, he is likely to avoid the area like the plague for weeks, and will completely alter his movement patterns. Their rugged adaptability will undoubtedly aid them through whatever future challenges they may face.

Changing climates may not severely damage their populations, however it will make them more difficult to harvest. Currently, climate change is the primary driver of whitetail expansion into non-native regions.[13] Warming climates lead to higher survival rates in deer population. This, however, is not a positive, as warmer seasonal cycles can lead to outbreaks of an infectious viral disease, called epizootic hemorrhagic disease, or EHD. Climate change is predicted to bring warmer summers, more severe winters, prolonged dry seasons, and heavier subsequent periods of rain. This environment is ideal for the transmission of EHD.[14] Referred to by hunters as Blue Tongue, EHD causes lethargy, weakness, swelling in the head and tongue, and internal bleeding. Further, warmer climates create a hotbed for the breeding and transmission of ticks. As climate change brings higher temperatures, especially in the American South, the spread of tick species will increase. There are currently eighteen tick species reportedly in contact with whitetail populations in the United States, which is already problematic. Increased tick populations will lead to higher disease transmission, infections, and anemia – and could cause tick-borne ailments to humans, such as Lyme disease. [15]

There is no definitive answer as to what effect climate change will have in the future. While climate change is out of the hands of the individual hunter, as a group we can work as one to ensure our own sacred hunting sites remain healthy for our own use, as well as that of future generations. The continuation of both ethical harvesting and respectful land conservation practices are key in nurturing healthy deer populations. The effects of a changing climate should be considered by grassroots organizations such as Backwoods Hunt Club. Already, the Club has a role in land conservation other than ethical hunting practices; scheduled off-season workdays to Club tracts allow members to clear old logging paths for ease of access and to fix water drainage issues on sloping roadbeds. Clear, full access to tracts allow members to field monitor activity year-round, to ensure that animal populations are healthy enough to harvest and that no trespassers are hunting illegally. Responsible hunters, like those in the Club, both nourish and study the landscape year-round to determine the best hunting tactics for deer season, and likely unknowingly act as conservationists in that regard. Further, stewardship of the lands in which our forefathers hunted and lived in is the best way to honor their memories, and to continue a shared way of life. As hunters, knowledge of our own personal histories in regard to our intangible heritage is among the most important aspects within the preservation of that heritage. The men in the

Royall family I know today, along with those I have known such as my uncle and great-grandfather, have been shaped by each generation of the Royall family as they travelled to and settled within North Carolina. To further our understanding of why we hunt and conserve, our past should be observed.

Built Environment, History, and Genealogical Records of the Royall Family

The majority of existing structures associated with the Royall family of the past lie in states of disrepair – a common characteristic of past homesteads in rural areas. Like most rural areas in the South, many old homesteads and barns in the area are in plain view from the roadside, nestled into the hillside, atop a ridge, or among dense trees. Today, they are more or less a visual backdrop, though there are those who do not grant them even that amount of significance. Modern society has no perceived use for them, and as such they are left in a state of neglected decay. They imbue a rustic character and charm to the area, though more importantly they are capable of telling the stories of the regions past - as all historic structures can do. Unfortunately, most landowners do not have the time, money, nor care to preserve said homesteads. Local history in rural areas is primarily oral, passed along by friend or family; often landowners do not know much of the history of homesteads on their land, unless it was built by past family. Because of this, rural history is personal; it is not widely shared, and can instill both pride and mystery regarding homestead sites. Only in recent years, with the ability to access large online databases, can these places be truly woven into a deeper historical context.

The Royall structures of the past are capable of telling the stories of our forefathers. What information that can be attained from each paint vivid images of their generational journey as immigrants to Jamestown, Virginia from England, to frontier homesteaders in western North Carolina. Small amounts of information can be gathered from individual generations; what can be gathered from each are pieced together to tell an overarching story, with themes of simplicity and living off the land. The lives of the Royall men in my family, such as my father, grandfather, and for a short time my great-grandfather, have each been shaped by the accumulation of knowledge passed down from generations of homesteaders, farmers, and hunters.

Doggams Plantation and Joseph Royall

While the Royall family can be traced clearly to farmers and leatherworkers in Essex, England, well into the 1400s, the family's significance in the Americas begins with Joseph Royall the Emigrant. Little is known of his birth c.1600 or youth in Essexshire, just outside of London other than his upbringing as a farmer. In 1622, at 20 years of age, Joseph immigrated to Virginia[16] on the ship *Charitie*. Historical records show him living in Charles City, Virginia, in 1623.[17] He began his time in the colonies as an indentured shipmaster for Luke Boyse, captaining Boyse's passenger ship between England and Virginia. In 1625, Luke's wife Alice Boyse and their four daughters accompanied Joseph Royall from England to Virginia. Somewhere along the way, Joseph, "'thru neglecte' [*sic*] caused sea water to ruin the clothing of the passengers".[18] This seems to have enraged Alice, as she proposed that Joseph remain permanently indentured to account for his mishap. Luke died shortly thereafter, and records show Mrs. Boyse petitioning a court in 1625, stating that Joseph was "…bound unto the said Luke Boyse to perform certain conditions therein mentioned…. Joseph Royall shall make or cause to be made gratis for the said Alice Boyse, her child and such servants as were then of this family…. till such day and time as he shall depart this land, so long as those of the family shall either serve her or the child."[19] There is no record of his continued servitude ever being enforced. It is unknown how Joseph evaded the proposed continued indentured servitude to the Boyse family. However, with Luke dead Joseph likely left on his own accord.

In 1637, Joseph is shown as a landowner in Charles City County, with 300 acres of land patented on the James River to the Isham-Royall plantation, known as "Doggams" today.[20] He was granted a hundred acres of land in Charles City County on the river sometime in the 1630s, and Joseph married Katherine Banks shortly thereafter.[21] By 1642, Joseph added 200 acres to his land on the southern shore of the James River, which he later sold. In 1642, he patented 600 acres along the river in Charles City County. He had a number of children with Katherine – two sons, Joseph Royall III, born around 1655, and John Royall, as well as three daughters - Sarah, Katherine, and one other who remains unnamed. He died on

March 10, 1655, in Charles City, Virginia, at the age of 53, and was buried there. Widowed Katherine Banks would later marry local landowner Henry Isham. Katherine's will bequeath "to my son Joseph Royall all my lands."[22] The will is detailed; however, it makes no mention of owned slaves. Given the seventeenth century era and size of the plantation, it is undeniable that indentured servants and enslaved Africans were present. However, there is no way to know for certain if African slaves were present unless some form of archaeological research were performed at the site.

Doggams plantation remained in the Royall family until 1929, when it was sold to James Pickney Harrison, a direct descendant of Katherine Banks-Isham and Henry Isham. It currently remains in the Isham family, and has been nominated by the Virginia Department of Historic Resources for listing on the National Register of Historic Places.[23] It is also part of the James River Plantations tourist organization, and is included on the Jamestown Discovery Trail – a heritage trail that encompasses the Charles City historic area.[24]

Doggams is the earliest known preserved structure belonging to the Royall family heritage. The structure at Doggams is a well-preserved, wooden L-shaped, two-story Colonial house. Historians of Colonial Williamsburg date it to the early 1700s following the death of Joseph, although family members insist it was built during his lifetime, between 1630 and 1650. Additions were made to the structure during the nineteenth century. Today, the structure is four bays wide and two bays deep on each length. There are three brick chimneys, a steep gable roof, and dormer windows spanning both lengths atop each bay. It has been a private residence since its construction.

Both Joseph the emigrant and Doggams plantation are important to the heritage of the Royall family for numerous reasons. Since Joseph is the first recorded Royall in North America, a vast number of Royall's within the United States can, and have, traced their lineage directly to him, including my own family. The Doggams plantation came into existence only a few decades after the founding of Jamestown in 1609 – the first settlement within the Virginia colony. While Joseph himself was a career farmer instead of a hunter or trapper (though he likely practiced both to some extent), his ability to connect with and understand his natural surroundings gave him success as an early colonial farmer in a largely unsettled area. While no Royall settlement would ever reach the size or monetary success of Doggams, Joseph began a tradition of homesteading and living with the land in the rural South for the Royall family.

Royall Family in North Carolina

Some of the Royall family resettled in Surry County, North Carolina, in the years following the Revolutionary War.[25] John Eppes Royall, the great-great grandson of Joseph the emigrant, was born in 1729 in Virginia,[26] though began his family homestead in the Mt. Airy region of North Carolina in the vicinity of Stone Mountain around 1800. Settlement of the area by those of European descent began sometime during the 1760s, though the Revolutionary War slowed migration southward.[27]

Mt. Airy was a frontier settlement that served as a rural trading post and stagecoach stop between Winston-Salem, North Carolina and Galax, Virginia. The settlement remained as such until the mid-eighteenth century, when it began its transition to a more agrarian-based economy.[28]

While the early Royall structures of the Mt. Airy region have unfortunately been lost to both time and jurisdiction of private property owners, they are comparable in historical context to the well preserved Hutchinson Homestead of Stone Mountain State Park. The homestead, built at the foot of the 600 foot granite face of Stone Mountain, was completed in its entirety during the mid-nineteenth century and inhabited through the 1950s.[29] It includes five individual structures; a log cabin, barn, blacksmith, corncrib, and meat house. It was opened to the public in 1998, and includes information that details life in the area during that period. Each structure is built in a vernacular Log Cabin style, with buildings made of hand-hewn and scored logs, stone chimneys stacked by hand, and red clay chinking between logs.[30] The homestead operated as a small, independent farm – they raised both livestock and crops for sustenance, along with what they could hunt in the area.[31] They lived with minimal possessions, and only valued what they truly needed. This was a material characteristic shared by frontier families, comparable to John Eppes Royall and the generations that followed him.

John Eppes Royall's will, written in 1810, lists the entirety of his property which was to be passed to his children. It included his house and land along with one cow and one hog to each of his four children, as well as one “shot gun” which would have been a traditional black powder musket. The will details one hundred acres of land in Rowan County, North Carolina, to be passed to his son, Joseph. Today, Rowan County is located in central North Carolina, just northeast of Charlotte. However, in 1771, Surry County was formed out of Rowan County which encompassed a greater portion of western North Carolina at the time.[32] The hundred acres of land in which the homestead was built is likely somewhere within the re-drawn Surry County, as Rowan County today is too far south to match records. Given the amount of historic log cabin structures that still stand in the Carolina countryside, it is possible that the physical remains of their homestead still exist. However, private property, dated records, and the sheer size of the countryside would make any effort to pinpoint its location all but futile.

The will also detailed the kitchenware down to each cast-iron skillet, pot, knife, fork, dish, and plate. From a modern perspective, it may seem peculiar that silverware or pots are included in someone’s will at all, much less that they make up nearly the entirety of it. However, when placed in the historical context of frontier homesteaders, these were the materials that allowed them to eat – in turn, guaranteeing their foreseeable survival. Politics and attributes of wealth, such as materialism, social trends, and styles of décor were ideas unknown to those living a frontier lifestyle. All that is left of John Eppe Royall’s legacy is his written 1810 will; while there is nothing else physical of his to preserve, the simplicity of the document’s contents defines the material culture of the family for many generations to come.

John Eppes' great-grandson, William Royall, was born in 1824 and moved southward with other family members following the death of his father Henry in 1828.[33] In 1851, the southern portion of Surry County in which they moved to was redrawn, and renamed Yadkin County – bordered by the Yadkin River to the north and east, and the Brushy Mountain's, a spur of the Blue Ridge range, to the west. The move of William Royall southward to Hamptonville in Yadkin County was the final major relocation of the Royall family, where they remained as homesteaders through the mid-twentieth century. William's grave can be found in the Center United Methodist Church Cemetery, or Old Center Cemetery, in Yadkinville.[34]

According to the 1860 U.S. Census, at 36 years old William Royall was a farmer with an estate valued at $346 – equivalent to roughly $10,783.44 today, given average yearly inflation rates of 2.17 percent since 1860. However, in the 1850 census, his total worth is recorded at $75 with no children.[35] He was married to Fannie Holcomb, and by 1860 they had five children.[36] William and his family worked their homestead in Hamptonville near the town of Yadkinville until his death in 1906, which had a population of approximately 120.[37] As a Yadkin County family homestead, they were self-sufficient. Other than salt, lead for bullets, paper, or coffee, all they would ever require was grown or derived from local raw materials. Yadkin homesteaders often grew both sweet and Irish potatoes, cabbage, onions, and local greens such as narrow dock, a type of buckwheat.[38] They also often had pear and walnut trees, along with corn and straw for livestock feed. Fruits, such as apples and Muscadine grapes, were often turned to cider or brandy. Houses, barns, corncribs, smokehouses, blacksmiths, and sometimes icehouses were typically built of hand cut and hewn pine, chinked with red clay, and elevated on platforms of stacked river stone. Trees of cedar, pine, and maple were often planted in close proximity to offer shade during the day. Yadkin homesteads and farmhouses typically were one-and-a-half stories, with glass windows and three to five rooms. Cooking was done over an open hearth, in a room laden with cast iron skillets, meat hooks, knives, and perhaps a Dutch oven. A room within the home or barn was reserved for tanning hides for leather, insulation, or blankets, next to a wheel where flax or cotton was spun to make clothing. Furniture, such as tables, chairs, and beds were made from readily available forest materials. Smokehouses smelled of hickory, fish from the Yadkin River, and game from the forest hung to cure. Most farms were 160 acres or less, and were managed by nuclear families with occasional hired assistance.[39]

William was not one of the 1,200 individuals of Yadkin County to join the Confederate ranks following the outbreak of the Civil War in 1861.[40] While Yadkin County may have no longer been a frontier by this point in the nineteenth century, it was still sparsely populated; culturally, it was similar to Appalachian mountain counties in that people lived in isolated pockets of close-related families.[41] Landowning yeoman farmers and homesteaders in the western part of the state tended to be less politically inclined, as they provided for their own needs on a day-to-day basis with little to no external interaction outside of their small communities. Further, western and eastern North Carolina were at a political contrast at the outbreak of the war. The eastern coastal plain had a long history of plantation class society, slave ownership, and aristocracy; in the hills to the west, only a select few wealthy landowners owned slaves, as the upcountry homesteaders that made up the region tended to be fiscally poor.[42] Yadkin County, along with other mountain counties, had a slave population of less than ten percent, whereas coastal counties had slave populations of fifty percent or greater.[43] Typical Yadkin landowners that were politically inclined tended to disagree with the Lowcountry and plantation class ideologies. Lower-income landowners felt that they were taxed too much, and that plantations were taxed too little. As most Yadkin landowners were non-slaveholding homesteaders, they held more influence within the local community. Many yeoman landowners felt that the Union protected them from potentially being bought or forced out by aristocratic classes and large-scale plantation owners. As such, the mountain counties and upcountry farmers tended to support the Union as there was not a ruling plantation presence. This is evidenced through North Carolina's reluctance to secede, as they were the second to last state to do so behind Tennessee. Western counties contributed in total 25,000 soldiers to the Union, and many Yadkin County Confederate conscripts often deserted.[44]

William Royall's family likely would not have survived had he left. At the outbreak of the war, he had five children under the age of ten, one of which was an infant.[45] High inflation rates drove up items such as bushels of corn from $1.10 to $30 by the end of the war,[46] and people began raiding one another's stockpiles of flour and corn. Often, Confederate currency was not accepted within the county.[47] From what records are available, it can be inferred that William fell into the category of those detached from the political sphere, as his priorities were providing for his family. Clearing land, butchering hogs, picking flax and cotton for clothing, plowing, planting crops, preserving foods, carrying water from the nearby spring, chopping wood; these tasks were all daily necessities, and likely could not be done alone by a woman trying to raising an infant. Brothers Willie D. Royall and Isaac Royall, cousins of William, living in the same community and of the similar age, served as a Private of Company F in the 28th Infantry Regiment of the Confederacy, and in Company A of the 1st Battalion Sharpshooters, respectively.[48] Willie was captured in 1863 at Amelia Courthouse in Virginia, and took an Oath of Allegiance to the United States, upon which he was released and returned home. Isaac Royall deserted in Greensborough, North Carolina, in 1864 after one month of conscription.[49]

The New South

Seldom told is the story of the man who cared not for wars, and aimed only to pull himself up by his bootstraps and to forge his own path. These people in the Old South were often yeoman farmers, tenant laborers, or hunters and trappers[50] far from aristocracy and the social elite. History tends to categorize those individuals, with terms rooted in the toils of their trade, that have come to hold negative connotation "redneck," "sandhiller," or more commonly, "cracker." Poor, Southern white individuals bore the brunt of the Civil War, as their homes were destroyed either by Union soldiers or rogue Confederate deserters,[51] and their labor was extorted to support a war effort that ultimately could not succeed. Thus, they were left in shambles, depleted of resources, and were branded with a negative connotation. [52] Consequently, poor Southerners remained relatively un-studied and stereotyped throughout the twentieth century as the world evolved around them. However, they represent a complex social and economic structure that has mostly been overlooked, and many post-Civil War setbacks can still be identified among rural Southern communities today.

Though economics in the South have changed, many individuals come from families that have remained in a position of dependency since the latter days of the rural Old South; landless tenants and poor farmers that do not have the resources to elevate their economic position to a higher status.[53] Reconstruction brought the emergence of industry and corporatism in urbanized areas, which often resulted in lackluster education, poor employment opportunities, and an evaporating tax base in rural communities. The root of these issues can be traced back to the Reconstruction era following the Civil War. In 1874 Henry W. Grady, a prominent newspaper editor in Atlanta, Georgia, described the

"New South" as an abandonment of agrarian economic practices, along with sharecropping and tenant farming, with modern replacement – such as factories, mines, mills, corporatization, and industrialism.[54] [55] Rural agrarian poverty in the South existed long before the Civil War, and many of those within the homesteading Royall lineage would have been considered financially impoverished. Following the War, sharecropping and tenant farming replaced slavery on Southern plantations, in which property owners acted as landlords in contract with impoverished laborers who would work for wages in the vacuum of slaves. Tenant famers received loans from landowners to purchase the required equipment and seeds. However, these farmers could not repay the loans following harvest periods, as cotton and tobacco prices were too low. This began a vicious cycle of poverty from indebtedness to landowners, which stifled the South's economy following the war.[56]

Henry W. Grady's depiction of the New South was spread through various publications and public speeches. In time, his promises gained traction among both Southern aristocracy and Northern investors.[57] He described the New South as "a perfect democracy... a social system compact and closely knitted, less splendid on the surface, but stronger at the core; a hundred farms for every plantation, fifty homes for every palace; and a diversified industry that meets the complex needs of this complex age."[58] He created a vision of a Southern economic utopia, elevated from the agrarian past through industrial manufacturing, urbanism, and commerce. However, many in the

South did not experience the industrial advancement that the Northern states did during the American Industrial Revolution, or Second Industrial Revolution, of the 1880s. The promise of dynamic economic change and growth failed to come to fruition in beneficial ways for average people within Southern cities and rural communities.

Reconstruction was not a total failure in terms of economic change, however; various industries, such as textile mills, ironworks, mines, and large manufacturing plants did emerge in the South. For example, North Carolina became the leading state in tobacco production. R.J. Reynolds Tobacco Company, founded in 1875 by R. J. Reynolds in Winston-Salem, is currently the second largest tobacco company in the Unites States. In 1875, Reynolds sold shares he held of his father's tobacco company in Patrick County, Virginia, and travelled by railroad to the emerging economic settlement of Winston-Salem, a small town of roughly 400 people. He purchased a factory building from the Moravian Church, and within his first year the company sold 150,000 pounds of tobacco – though by the 1890s the company was exporting over a million pounds per year.[59] The factory buildings were both the largest and most advanced in Winston-Salem, with steam and electric power. By 1916, Reynolds Tobacco had elevated Winston-Salem to the eighth largest port of entry in the United States.[60] As Winston-Salem became a hub of commerce, people from the surrounding countryside began commuting or relocating from rural communities for employment. Commerce within smaller nearby towns, such as

Yadkinville, simply could not compete. The landscape, which had been untouched save for small independent farmers, would be transformed into vast tobacco fields for mass harvest and export.

Prosperity for factory owners and tenant landlords was the extent of Grady's promise of a New South. Sharecroppers remained in a cycle of debt, and low wage factory work kept individuals of lower financial classes from ascending the rapidly evolving socioeconomic ladder. Those living in poverty within rural areas who were promised a way out through industrialization were eventually denied that promise. Rising property taxes, post-war inflation, and the day to day demands of living in a society growing increasingly complex remained factors contributing to rural poverty. Among these economic changes, the New South brought about change to rural cultural landscapes that had previously remained relatively uninterrupted for well over a century. Increased economic and social interconnectedness placed a higher demand on self-sustaining homesteaders. Miles Shelah Royall, referred to as Shelah and called "Papaw Shelah" by my father, was born in Hamptonville in Yadkin County on July 20, 1896. He was the youngest of seven children born to William and Emma Royall.

Tobacco production had become the cash crop of the region – his father was among the last generation of homesteading, self-sufficient farmers. By Shelah's young adulthood in the 1910s, the landscape of western North Carolina could no longer be characterized by dense pine forest with homesteads hidden within. Much of the wilderness had been stripped bare to reveal rolling hills coated in green tobacco leaves, dotted with tobacco barns. Shelah spent much of his youth working tobacco fields along with his siblings. Self-sufficient homesteading families could no longer sustain themselves by working their owned land alone; increased socioeconomic demand required each family member to make a financial contribution. The majority of the tobacco fields in Yadkin County either were owned by or sold their crop to RJ Reynolds by the twentieth century. The company employed nearly 10,000 people within its Winston-Salem factories; however, the number of individuals who worked in fields in surrounding counties is immeasurable.[61] While this gave those in rural areas an opportunity for employment, the cutting period for tobacco plants only lasts six weeks out of the year after the plants transition from a deep green to a golden-brown. Working tobacco fields was laborious, time-consuming, and not financially lucrative enough to elevate field workers socioeconomically. Congruent with the promises of the New South, industrialized agriculture only brought about real beneficial change to the land and factory owners.

Industrializing agriculture made hunting the local landscape increasingly difficult. Large plots of land had been divided, and private property lines became real boundaries. The freedom to hunt and track unabated was fading. The disturbance of clearing land drove whitetail west, higher into the mountains. Further, due to its heavy metals and toxins, deer do not eat tobacco plants. Thus, the population in North Carolina all but vanished as natural food sources became scarce. Historically, homesteaders would slaughter their livestock for food on the basis of necessity – hunting was their fundamental means of subsistence. However, as the world around them became more industrialized, those with a prior dependence on hunting had no choice but to adapt to those changes. The dollar became more important in day-to-day life, and the cultivation of one's well-being became something that had to be bought.

Illicit Ventures

Due to the short duration of the tobacco harvesting season, Shelah Royall, along with other family and community members, had no choice but to turn to more lucrative financial ventures. When my family began distilling and bootlegging illicit un-aged whiskey, or moonshine, is unknown - though Shelah likely began assisting in his father's operation as soon has he was old enough to learn the skill. Distilling corn whiskey had been a century-long tradition in the western hill counties of Surry, Wilkes, Yadkin, as well as in the mountain counties. The tradition of distilling whiskey was originally one of Scottish and Irish immigrants in the region. However, Irish and Scottish whiskey was distilled from peat, grain, and honey. In order to continue distillation in North America, immigrants were required to have a relationship with German and English growers of corn and rye,[62] which resulted in the shared knowledge of distilling whiskey along with the diffusion of the culture in the Carolina frontier.

North Carolina's Prohibition of the sale of alcohol began on May 26, 1908 - though certain aspects, such as independent distribution, had technically been illegal for years. Prior to, during, and even after the Prohibition era, the distillation and transportation (or bootlegging) of illegal whiskey often was the single most important factor in keeping a family from starving. Even as an illegal offense, it remained an essential economic contributor within Appalachian communities. The process of moonshine distillation is tedious, strenuous, and exhaustive. During the Prohibition era, it was routinely done overnight as to diminish the potential of being caught; however, the coolness of the night air is beneficial for the distillation process. Often, it was a family business; women acted as lookouts and local bootleggers, delivering to neighbors, and younger boys assisted in distillation.[63] During Prohibition, those within Yadkin County typically had their distilleries hid among the Brushy Mountains to the west, near the Wilkes County line, as the rough mountain terrain was difficult to access and navigate. It was within these mountains to the west of Hamptonville where Shelah spent countless nights in the woods, by a creek, stirring corn in steaming water over his moonshine still until the sunrise.

Western North Carolina's moonshine culture continued to rise after the conclusion of America's Prohibition era. By the 1950s, highway systems had allowed for diversified means of transportation. Some of the original bootlegging haulers, such as Junior Johnson, born in neighboring Wilkes County in 1931, became instrumental in the founding of NASCAR[64] as well as a star within the sport; Johnson is responsible for popularizing for the now-common phrase "good ol' boy," which at the time epitomized respected bootlegger within moonshine culture.[65] By the 1950s, neighboring Wilkes County had been referred to as the moonshine capital of the world by some journalists – a title that enraged "upstanding" members of society - and bootleggers in the region could make thousands of dollars a week hauling to Charlotte, Wilkesboro, Winston-Salem, and elsewhere.[66]

Remnants of Moonshine Culture

Shelah's Prohibition-era still currently rests in my grandfather's barn in Hamptonville. Local authorities would track down moonshine stills in the hillside, plant dynamite inside, ignite the dynamite, and destroy them. Moonshiners distilled liquor at night to avoid capture, as the steam from a still could be seen from a distance in the light. They were often not caught at their stills, as raids took place during the day. Though we already know the age of his still, it can be proven to be undoubtedly of Prohibition era due to the dynamite craters in its hull. At some point, lawmen found it and destroyed it; years later, my grandfather, Bud, returned to the mountain creek where it was left to retrieve it. The destruction of Shelah's still did not mark the end of the Royall family's days of 'shining. Shelah passed the tradition to his son Hubert Jennings, who in turn passed it to my grandfather.

Following a long day of successful hunting, tracking, and cleaning of a deer, we sit in my grandfather's semi-basement in Hamptonville and shared a few sips out of a jar. To this day, my grandfather brews various liquors in an assortment of flavors, such as apple-pie brandy or blueberry moonshine. Behind his house, a short walk down the hillside towards the creek, one might find an upside-down wheelbarrow with an old apple barrel underneath. Within that apple barrel might just be a stash of moonshine. Often while we are dressing and skinning deer in the evening, my grandfather will disappear down the hill, and emerge a few minutes later with a jar in hand to share. Countless evenings have been spent skinning animals and sipping moonshine, long before I was of the age to partake. My grandfather tells stories of Papaw Hubert's days dodging the law, business dealings (and subsequent friendship) with Junior Johnson, and distilling until the early hours of the morning. Many stories and laughs shared remain the same over time, though the people present have changed; now, we recall fond memories of my late uncle Jeff, with stories from within my lifetime and before.

The unlicensed distillation of moonshine for commercial sale remains illegal; however, local police often do not pursue it. The market is no longer the same in rural areas. Small, local distillers still exist in the countryside that typically distill for personal consumption. Issues of cocaine and prescription drug abuse, as well as the emergence of liquor stores in the latter half of the twentieth century drove big moonshine operations into urban areas, which were often consolidated into legal distilleries. Independent distilling surely is not what it used to be, and the commercialization of moonshine has removed the process from its cultural roots. However, there are still those such as my grandfather that distill independently – a small act of civil disobedience that is a testament to our forefathers. Today, small stills can be purchased along with necessary equipment, and enthusiasts have the ability to network with one another via the Internet. Moonshining may not ever be what it once was, for good reason; however, small, local distillers such as my grandfather do their part in keeping the tradition alive. The preservation of hunting is one in the same; the best we can do to preserve it is to do our part locally.

Conclusion

Today, hunting is vastly different. We no longer set out from the porch of our wooden cabin, scanning immediately for tracks in soft ground or for scrapes on low trees. When we listen over the sound of the breeze, we may hear the sound of cars passing on a nearby road, the barking of dogs echoing through the hollow, or the sound of heavy agricultural machinery. We return from the hunt to warm, insulated homes, heated by modern HVAC systems; homes that are built with a foundation of concrete, and a veneer of brick and stucco. At night, we sit around a fire lit with a lighter and fluid burning from logs cut by chainsaw, piled high in only a few short hours. Our lives are quickly-paced, and we often hunt with undue urgency that causes eventual mistakes. Our forefathers had the ability to hunt with patience; to them, the looming prospect of a day of driving back home after a week of hunting was nonexistent. They did not set game cameras in the woods and navigate with hand-held GPS devices, nor did they have week-long weather forecasts to determine the best days to hunt. They hunted simply, and simply hunted. Small glimpses into our past still exist; the homestead my great-grandfather built, the tools he and his family used, such as my great-grandfather's hunting knife and turtle trap, and my great-great grandfather's moonshine still offers us depictions of what their lives were like. They led lives of simplicity, though they endured many hardships. The material things they used shed light on times long past, and allow us to remember them as we follow in their footsteps. Perhaps the most effective method in preserving hunting is through memories. Memories we have made with one another along with those we have of our family's past drive us into the woods year after year. Those memories can be shared in meaningful ways with friends both old and new, seasoned hunters or beginners. We can continue to chase the nostalgia of being outside; the scent of the crisp mountain air, the cool breeze we feel at our faces that rustles the leaves overhead, and the feeling of a successful hunt can be preserved through proper stewardship and conservation of our hunting lands. An understanding of our ancestors gives us a deeper connection to hunting and our natural surroundings. I share all of this with my father, grandfather, and great-grandfather, all of whom have shared it with their fathers and grandfathers – a cycle of shared memories that spans a dozen generations in North Carolina that will be passed on to the next in time.

Epilogue

…. In the moments following chaos, I watch as the group of deer scramble away from the field towards the pine thicket. My heart thumps heavy in my chest, and my breath feels short as I watch the buck bound towards the tree line. With his white tail flapping like a flag of surrender, he disappears into the darkness of the brush in one great leap. Shortly after, my cell phone vibrates in my pocket. “You get him?” my father asks. “I think so,” I respond, though I question my shot, wondering if I pulled my aim too far to my right, or if I underestimated the distance between myself and the buck. The group of nearby deer seems to have either forgotten about the gunshot, or realized they were not at the receiving end; they leap about for a short time, then stop to continue their grazing in the field. Time passes, and the sun rises higher, burning away the fog and providing light for the coming day. I rise and meet my father in the field as I try to recall where the buck stood. We begin scanning the ground, and find signs of blood and disturbed earth. We follow it faintly, and determine where he entered the thicket. We duck in cautiously, crouching underneath limbs of trees, catching our thick clothing in briars and thorns. The presence of heavy blood and organ matter on the leaves indicates we are close. We follow the trail into a pine hammock, and find the buck lying on its side, lifeless – the shot was clean through the lungs. I crouch next to the animal and run my hand across its side, admiring the rugged beauty of it while accepting the bitterness of taking a life. For now, the hunt is over; the work to haul it out, clean it, and prepare it to eat has only just begun.

Chapter 4: Raised on Religion: The Preservation of Religious Cultural Heritage of a Family

By Martha Stegall

Religious cultural heritage is important in understanding the spirituality, morals, and traditions of a Church and its community. It can explain the motives of the daily choices such as movement patterns, location, and underlying factors that give reason to the way a community is shaped. This includes the preservation of the material and intangible aspects of religion, such as the physical church, rituals, and beliefs. As this type of preservation increases, the desire to visit these places on pilgrimage also increases, encouraging others to participate as well. The preservation of the Church's structure gives visitors the opportunity to visually see the past and where it took place. This is the most common and simplest form of religious cultural preservation. However, the religious heritage of a church and community is not accurately preserved without the associated intangible beliefs and traditions. The successful preservation of religious cultural heritage requires the inclusion of congregational records, the physical church, and documenting the beliefs of participants.

The preservation of religious heritage is not limited to the church system; it can also be practiced by individual families. This gives the family the opportunity to understand their history, morals, and evolving beliefs of their ancestors.

Through this, a family can then better understand the driving factors and reasons behind the choices of their ancestors and continue these traditions into the future, if desired.

Many aspects of life influence family tradition and practices. The choices made by our ancestors influences the way families will be in the future. Ideally, we are predestined for a good life because on the life choices of those before us. For my case, this includes my ancestor's choice of Christianity and their inclusion of it in their daily lives, which serves as a foundation of faith. Ideologies set expectations on personal, family, and communal morals. For instance, my mother's only guidelines for her children seeking a potential spouse are:

1. They must treat their mother well (shows respect to women and parents),
2. They must know how to fix a toilet (evidence of resourcefulness, as well as a strong parent-figure in their life), and
3. They must love Jesus.[1]

Growing up, these three things were jokingly repeated into my sister's and my head. These may sound silly or non-important to most; however, they contain a deeper meaning that reflects upon my family's morals through past generations. Christian beliefs are subconsciously embedded into my family and makes us the way we are. It influences the way children are raised, family traditions, moral compass, and how we interact with others. Even though contemporary religious beliefs are not identical with those of our ancestors, the choice of religion from our ancestors explains the characteristics of my family today.

Religion has been and continues to be the main influencer in the choices of my family. Throughout time, my family has passed down heritage records and stories, which reveal the significance of Christianity to our ancestors. By preserving these records and the stories from the past, we can take a glimpse into our ancestor's lives, study how religion has affected their choices, and gain an understanding on why my family is the way that it is today. Through the practice of preservation and the continuation of religious faith, my family heritage stays alive. We can continue their legacy by mirroring their ethics in our decisions today. Preservation work in my family, such as family research, the passing down of stories, the continuous recording of family information, and the continuation of Christianity preserves our family heritage. This intentional preservation of religious beliefs and morals is vital to the preservation of our religious cultural heritage allowing for the beliefs of our ancestors to be carried through generations.

Preservation of Religious Heritage

The preservation of religion is widely used around the world to preserve the cultural heritage of communities. As the desire to visit religious places and pilgrimage grows, the yearning to preserve these sites and experience the community heritage around these places simultaneously grows. The most common form of this is the preservation of the physical church. However, the preservation of religious practice is key to the preservation of the church, because it gives cultural meaning and significance to why these places matter. To achieve a proper preservation of religious heritage, it is very as important to take into account the views and opinions of the specific community in question. This includes the involvement of the youth in preservation decisions. The preservation of religious heritage includes outsider pilgrimage, the Church's involvement, and community involvement in decision-making to accurately portray the significance of the physical and spiritual church.

Religion is one of many components to a culture that makes its unique and can give a community or place its cultural and historical significance. According to Avi Astor, Marian Burchardt, and Mar Griera, religion "is a set of shared beliefs and behaviors for interacting with divine forces and orienting oneself to follow the teachings or dictates of a particular worldview. But in practice, religion is often so much more than that—it is a shared 'style of life' that shapes meanings and behaviors of both the sacred and profane."[2] Religious heritage consists of places, but also specific beliefs and ritual practices.[3] By intertwining the tangible with the intangible, religious heritage can be accurately and effectively preserved. Tangible objects include sacred places as well as ritual objects and relics.[4] Intangible aspects of entail oral traditions and rituals, as well as even sacred landscapes or vistas.[5]

Religious cultural preservation is challenging and can be controversial due to conflicting opinions on faith. In order to recognize any place as significant, it is crucial to recognize the specific components that give it importance and make it different from the rest. Since "the religious character of certain elements may justify the application of special rules of protection, particularly in cases of sites or places marked with an exceptional religious gravity and unique historical importance" it is key to preserve the religion by the continuation of practices and traditions along with the preservation of the property.[6] However, it is difficult to define what is significant and what is not, due to the fact that some religious beliefs and practices could be significant to some and not to others because of different beliefs. The tangible aspects included in religious cultural preservation are religious monuments such as statues, groups of religious buildings, and religious sites such as landscapes.[7] None of which include the intangible evidence of a culture but only the tangible. It is the non-material essence of place that makes it significant, and should therefore be considered for preservation too.

Due to the significance religion holds to the audience of the religious public, visiting religious sites such as churches have become more popular. Faith-based travel is a global phenomenon, with religious pilgrimages dating back to ancient times.[8] As a result, the topic of religion is becoming very popular in the world of preservation. Currently there are over 95,000 properties on the National Register of Historic Places; over 107 of these properties are churches, among more that are sacred to other religions outside of Christianity.[9] Religious tourism encompasses the tangible aspects such as the church property as well as the intangible aspects of emotion and spiritually of visitors. The cultural attraction to the interest in visiting religious sites includes the ambiance, the condition of the area, and the significance connected to the culture. [10] To effectively represent the significance of the religion of a region "it is necessary to have a religious heritage."[11] To be more specific, this includes "material and immaterial components of the identity…" thus connecting the community to the property by including the preservation of the physical church and the practices and beliefs in which the community of the church contained.[12] Religious tourism gives the church's community their own opportunity to preserve their religious heritage and continue their legacy. If a church has a high number of visitors, it can better announce promote its moral and religious message.[13]

The preservation of religious cultural heritage can be seen within the church system itself, which gives the community and visitors the opportunity to understand the church's historical background and theology throughout time. A report from 1965 states "without going into too great detail one may safely say that there are in North America over 500 depositories of church historical materials. This indicates that there has been lively concern and interest on the part of the various denominations in providing for the preservation of records."[14] Since the topic of religion can be controversial to the public, and not everyone shows interest in it, it is important for each congregation to preserve its heritage to ensure the information is available in the future. The material being preserved in these depositories includes but is not limited to church specific historical materials and archival and manuscript materials.[15] "Some depositories traditionally have been associated with theological seminary libraries whereas others trace their beginnings to semi-independent historical societies that gradually received certain official responsibilities."[16] While these types of information are effective in the preservation of a church's past, it is important to recognize the historical background of the community's theology taught within the congregation to fully preserve the religious cultural heritage. The church system plays a key role in the preservation of religious cultural heritage by collecting their own archival evidence for the public to understand the church and its impact on the community.

Community involvement in the preservation of religious heritage is crucial to understand the church's significance. Since the church was made for and by the people, one can conclude that it would hold no significance without them and their contributions and beliefs. The church provides the community a safe place to worship, feeding the spiritual heart of the community.[17] The youth involvement in the preservation of religious heritage is vital to the continuation and survival of the heritage. The involvement of the youth in preservation decisions is important as it familiarizes future generations who will be in charge of these decisions in the future with the ins and outs of cultural preservation. The United Nations Convention on the Rights of the Child in 1989 recognized a community's youth as an important stakeholder group in planning.[18] This allows for younger generations to partake in their own cultural and religious heritage and gives them power to create change and make contributions. "If we consider church spaces as significant to the physiological well-being of a community, as these places contribute fundamentally to a sense of place and belonging, then it follows that we have to ensure the community's views are actively sought in the identification of heritage assets".[19] Therefore, failing to recognize community youth as important, the views of the community become skewed and inaccurate. In the case of my family's religious heritage, the passing down of information, stories, and practices is a positive encouragement for youth participation in preserving our family heritage.

Religion is an evolving topic in the preservation world and strives to preserve religious properties is becoming more apparent. To achieve this, the participants must "identify best methods to support an in depth knowledge of the religious and cultural heritage, both tangible and intangible, and select the most suitable technical and management criteria for a proper conservation and enhancement of such heritage."[20] More and more religious sites, such as churches, are being placed on the National Register for Historic Places as a result of the public's growing desire to visit these places. Along with this growing interest of history and preservation of religious sites comes the challenge of recognizing the significance of a church and how to properly preserve the religious heritage of the church's region and community. Preservation of these sites gives the typical professionals of the preservation world, such as museums and heritage professionals, the challenge of reconciling "contemporary standards with practice in cases where religious communities are directly involved."[21] These challenges are often generated by the "existence of very different value systems" of the public.[22] Therefore it is crucial for the individual church to contribute to its own preservation and preservation of its heritage and legacy. By collecting church historical resources in depositories, the community is given the opportunity to take its religious cultural preservation into its own hands. However, "weakness in communication or public relations has become apparent with respect to most of the depositories for religious resources."[23] Therefore, community involvement is vital to the religious heritage by giving the information the emotional and spiritual attachment that visitors desire. The inclusion of all members of a church community is the most effective way to preserve this heritage. This inclusion encourages youth participation, which later passes down the religious heritage and also places the importance of this heritage into the hearts and minds of later generations, ensuring the continuation of the community's religious legacy. The successful preservation of communal religious cultural heritage relies on the entire community's participation, recognizing the tangible and intangible as significant together.

Why did my family move?

The importance of religion in my family dates back to the eighteen century and influenced the reasoning behind my ancestor's move to Kentucky from Virginia. My maternal ancestor, John Bush, came to Virginia on the ship *Neptune* in 1618. After some years in Virginia, the family grew to include the grandson of John Bush who is also named John Bush, along with his son Phillip. Phillip Bush had children of his own; Phillip Jr. William (Captain Billy Bush), Ambrose, Francis and sister Mary Richards. Between 1755 and 1790, Virginia experienced an abundance of religious revivalism, particularly Baptism, which changed the dynamics of the colony.[24] Baptists were often more disciplined, publicly aired their personal sins, and actively disciplined themselves of those sins. Thus, Baptism was a more publicly expressed faith compared to Anglicanism. Some Baptist practices went against those of the Church of England, which caused new converts to be labeled as lawbreakers. It was at times problematic to be Baptist in Virginia; therefore many of the Baptist faith to relocated.

Some members of the Baptist church opposed also slavery and encouraged enslaved Africans to worship with them. [25] This created conflict because the traditional Anglican Church believed that permitting enslaved Africans to attend church meetings would incite them to revolt.[26] As a result, Reverend Lewis Craig and Captain Billy Bush were persecuted for their contrary religious beliefs. As evangelical Baptism spread throughout Virginia, tensions rose due to the challenges to traditional dogma. During the 1770s, Daniel Boone, among others, began surveying land in Kentucky for settlement. In 1775, my ancestor Captain William (Billy) Bush, joined Daniel Boone in surveying the land and assisted in creating a route to a newly settled town known as Boonesborough.[27] During the excursion, Captain Bush was drawn to the land they were surveying, and so a group of family and neighbors in Virginia followed him to Kentucky. By November 1784, my family along with other Virginians, began to settle in Kentucky under the leadership of Captain Billy Bush.[28] The Baptist settlers were referred to as the "traveling church" believing "Heaven is a mere Kentucky of a place."[29] The 500 Baptists settlers viewed their migration to Kentucky as akin to that of the ancient Israelites crossing the wilderness from Egypt to the Promise Land.[30] This is how my family ended up creating the Bush Settlement in Kentucky, which remained in my family for generations to come.

The Bush Settlement & Old Stone Meeting House

After fleeing from Virginia for freedom of worship, Capitan Bush settled the group in an area north of the Kentucky River near Boonesborough in 1784, called the Bush Settlement.[31] A portion of the land was given to each member of the group, including several of my ancestors, where they built homes and farms. Along with this division of land was a parcel designated for a church. The Providence Church, also referred to as the Old Stone Meeting House, was erected in 1793 by the people of the Bush Settlement to practice their form of Christianity more freely. The Old Stone Meeting House Church was built in a valley off an early extension of the Old Wilderness Road, near Lower Howard's Creek, between Boonesborough and

Strode's Station. This site is currently called Winchester. Old Wilderness Road was mapped by Daniel Boone in 1771 and completed by his team, including Captain Bush in 1775. It begins in the southwest corner of Virginia and runs along the Tennessee River.[32] This road became a prominent path of travel for settlers as it provided access to areas such as the Shenandoah Valley and the James River in Virginia, and the New River in North Carolina.[33] The road ran through Virginia, North Carolina, and Kentucky by way of the Cumberland Gap. This gave my ancestors the opportunity to relocate in large groups, such as the traveling churches, and lead to the creation of new settlements in Kentucky.

The intentional placement of the Old Stone Meeting House Church reflected the settler's desire to openly practice their faith without persecution and to spread Christianity to others. Along with the intention to spread Baptism, the church was built from materials directly from the local environment. By placing the church in the valley, the surrounding hills protected the congregants from Native American attacks, which were still a threat to settlers. Although violent tensions with Native Americans subsided at the time of the congregation's establishment, fear from attacks, such as the Siege of Boonesborough in 1778, influenced the design and placement of the church.

The church's physical appearance portrays the surrounding environment, which ties with the area. The structure is constructed from local stone from a nearby cliff, known as Kentucky Marble. Kentucky Marble is a white limestone sedimentary rock that gives the illusion of marble due to its polished finish. The original church interior included "hand-hewn white ash boards nailed to the large oak joists with old iron nails suspected to be made by a local blacksmith and the interior walls were mud daubed and hand-made poplar wooden benches."[34] As the area became more populated, the use of local materials allowed settlers to build their community quickly and in-expensively. By using Kentucky Marble and the nails from the local blacksmith, the church physically ties together the settler's desire for a new place of worship and the environment of the Bush Settlement for future generations to observe. The Old Stone Meeting House is a tangible connection to my ancestors at Bush Settlement, reflecting the importance of faith and community on the old Kentucky frontier, and is listed on the National Register of Historic Places.

Figure 4.1: Postcard of the "Old Stone Meeting House" Church Building, Winchester, Kentucky, c.1920s. From the personal collection of the editor.

Studying Religion through Family Records

The keeping of family records is important to the preservation of family heritage as it allows us to go back in time and understand the influences of ancestral choices revealing a theme throughout time. Maintaining family records also gives the opportunity to continue the legacy of ancestors by providing a guideline to their beliefs. Not only does the use and examination of family documents passed down through generations preserve the family history, it also preserves the heritage by encouraging interest in the family's past. The practice of recording religious documents and reusing them in the future is one way my family preserves our own religious cultural heritage. My family participates in the preservation of our ancestral past by keeping a Family Book, containing records of each family member.

In the Family Book, hand drawn diagrams, called biblical typologies, created by my great-grandfather, William Clayton Rutledge, document the importance of Christianity in my family, as well as give insight into the beliefs of our family members at the time. Biblical typologies can be used to "interpret post-biblical events as following biblical patterns."[35] As "Typological interpretation has important theological implications," the examination and analysis of these documents provide a further and deeper understanding of the morals of my ancestors.[36] One example a typology found in the Family Book is a diagram labeled "The Golden Candlestick and the Bible" created on April 12, 1922. Rutledge also includes the wisdom of pastor, H.H. Adamson, from a sermon.

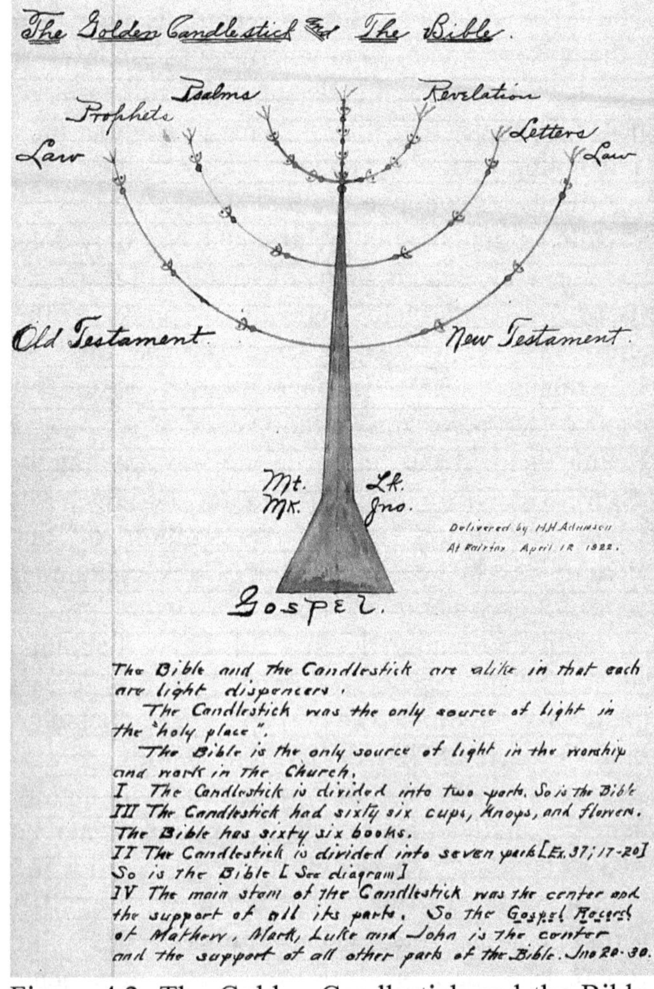

Figure 4.2: The Golden Candlestick and the Bible, dating from April 12, 1922 by William Clayton Rutledge. From the Family Book, the personal collection of the author.

On the page is a drawing of a candlestick with six branches reaching out with biblical references. Rutledge uses this candlestick diagram as a metaphor to the Bible stating, "the Bible and the Candlestick are alike in that each are light dispensers."[37] He explains that the candlestick was the only source of light in the "holy place" and the Bible is the only source of light in the worship and work of the Church. The candlestick is divided into two parts, labeled as the Old Testament and the New Testament. This is a reflection of the Bible as it is also divided into the two testament parts within the Baptist canon. The Candlestick has sixty-six cups, knobs, and flowers. He relates this to the Bible by explaining that the Bible has sixty-six books. The candlestick is also divided into seven parts, which represent the seven different parts of the Bible. The main stem of the candlestick is the center and support for all other parts, which is labeled as the Gospel. If taken into context, Rutledge is implying that the Gospel Record of the books Matthew, Mark, Luke, and John are the center and support all other parts of the Bible. This diagram documents my ancestor's belief that the Candlestick is the source of light in life, creating a religious symbol spanning generations.

The next page of the Family Book contains a second diagram of biblical typology by William Clayton Rutledge, based on another sermon by pastor H. H. Adamson in April 1922. It is labeled at "The Golden Chain of Life." The "chain" is separated into three different sections, "The Human Side" at the bottom, "The Divine Side'" at the top, and the "Gospel" in the center, connecting the two.

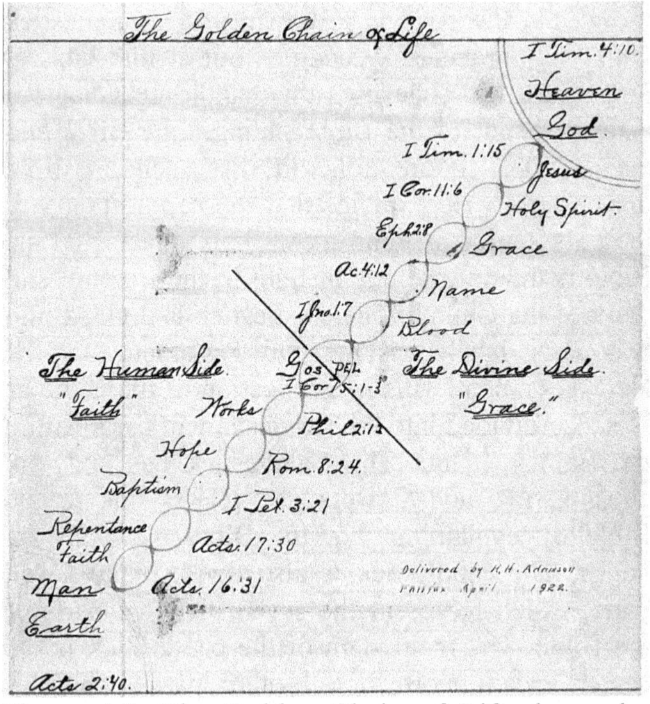

Figure 4.3: The Golden Chain of Life drawn by William Clayton Rutledge, based on a sermon given by H. H. Adamson in April 1922. From the Family Book, the personal collection of the author.

The chain diagram represents the interaction of Earth and Man, with Heaven and God, making the Gospel the meeting point between the two. This implies that the Gospel is what connects us with God. On each side, Rutledge wrote words that both man and God must contribute in order to live a faith-based life. Along the "Human Side" is the word faith, implying that we as humans must have faith in the Gospel and Christianity in order to continue the "chain" of life. Along the chain are specific words such as "Repentance, Baptism, Hope, and Works," with correlating biblical scripture quotes that explain the role of each word in the chain. For example, the word "Repentance" correlates to the scripture reading "And the times of this ignorance God winked at, but now commandeth all men everywhere to repent."[38] Together, these words give a guideline that we as people must do in order to continue the chain of life to reach God with scripture evidence. The "Divine Side" of the chain represents God's "Grace" that he has given us. The words associated with this side include "Blood", "Name," "Grace," "Holy Spirit," and "Jesus." Similar to the Human Side, Rutledge also correlates each word with scriptural evidence. For example, he correlates "Grace" with the scripture reading "For grace are ye saved through faith; and that not of yourselves: it is the gift of God."[39]

Together, Rutledge represents the words on one side of the chain as things God will give to humans, supported by biblical scripture. In the center, the Gospel connects "The Human Side" and the "Divine Side." Rutledge indicates the scripture reading "Moreover, brethren, I declare unto you the gospel which I preached unto you, which also ye have received, and wherein ye stand; by which also ye are saved, if ye keep in memory what I preached unto you, unless ye have believed in vain. For I deliver unto you first of all that which I also received, how that Christ died for our sins according to the scriptures."[40] This biblical typology explains the connection between humans and God and what each side is linked to the Gospel, supported by biblical texts. This diagram acts as a visual guideline to the practice of Christianity for my family. The inclusion of these biblical typologies in our Family Book shows the importance of Christianity for our ancestors. As "typology preserves the historicity of the prefiguring events," family morals and values can be carried over from one generation to the next.[41] This documentation is a fundamental example of my family's religious cultural heritage being preserved so that future generations, such as myself, can practice the same beliefs of our ancestors.

Preservation in my Family

Family heritage preservation can be in many forms such as a record book kept up to date, research done by family members, oral histories, and the passing down of information as a tradition. The preservation of religious family heritage relies on the preservation of family archives to provide key moralistic beliefs and traditions for future continuation. This also emphasizes the importance and sentimentality of heritage by creating a desire and excitement to learn about the past. For instance, family history creates an emotional attachment to the information shared and encourages other members of the family to contribute their own experiences. This transforms the practice of preservation into a family tradition that sustains it.

The continuous recording of information through time keeps the history of a family alive and gives the opportunity to relate to one's ancestors. In the case of the Family Book, younger generations can gain firsthand knowledge of ancestral information with less risk of misinterpreting information from oral histories. The Family Book is a primary source from our ancestors and is filled with pages of names, who they married, and their children, to which future children will add their names too. The book also contains important documents, such as the division of land in the Bush Settlement, detailing and mapping the plots of land that each family member owned at a point in history. This gives a visual understanding of the spatial relationship between people within the community. The hand drawn biblical typologies attach an emotional connection to ancestral faith and allows later generations to find similarities between past and present family beliefs.

Along with keeping family in the Family Book, we have also worked to find religious heritage through our own historical research on the past. In December 1975, Mary Cronan from the Kentucky Heritage Commission, nominated the Old Stone Meeting House Church to the National Register for Historic Places.[42] Cronan used sources, such as a map of the Bush Settlement, to "show how that Baptist colony of pioneer days, settled around the Old Stone Meeting House (Providence) as a nucleus."[43] The map also exhibited in large type the farm owners from before 1800. This particular map was made from Surveys and County Court records of Clark County, Kentucky, by S. J. Conkwright and Samuel Hodgkin Rutledge, my great-great uncle.[44] As a result of his work, the Old Meeting House Church could be successfully nominated to the National Register for Historic Places. Along with Samuel Hodgkin Rutledge, my great-grandfather William Clayton Rutledge, also contributed towards preservation work. He was awarded the "Master Conservationist Honor" at the Clark County Soil Conservation district Meeting.[45] Included in his work are descriptions of his land on the Bush Settlement and Conservation Plan Maps. Work done by Samuel Hodgkin Rutledge and William Clayton Rutledge led to additional preservation success at the Bush Settlement.

Documentation of the land plots at the Bush Settlement were also passed down through generations in conjunction with oral histories. Verbal story telling is an act of cultural preservation and further preserves the family heritage by keeping it alive. My mother recalls her childhood visits and memories to the family farm, which at the time was owned by my great-grandfather William Clayton Rutledge. For my mother, this was a direct tie to her ancestors by having tangible evidence of the past and stories passed down to her. While at the farm, her grandfather would frequently take her around the property and her Uncle Sam's property, which was also a part of the original Bush Settlement.

Exploration around the farm made learning about heritage fun for younger family members and instilled interest in the past and preservation into the minds of the younger generations. As a child, my mother recalls exploring around the properties finding evidence of those who were there before her. She would explore caves on the farm once used by Native Americans, collecting arrowheads and other artifacts as a reminder of the life challenges our ancestors faced. Artifacts from our family were also found and still being used today in the same fashion. For example, an iron skillet from my great uncle

Sam was passed down unto my mother. She continues to use the skillet to prepare the same type of meals her grandfather cooked for her on the farm as a child, passing on culinary traditions.

My mother recalls having these similar living conditions at the farm during her childhood in the 1970s as today. There was no running water at the house on the farm; they had to pump the water and bring it inside. Baths were given in the family wash tub that was also passed down from generation to generation. By using these artifacts in a similar way and having similar conditions to those of our ancestors, my mother was able to experience an emotional connection and deeper understanding of the lives of our ancestors. My mother also recalls religious practices during her visits. It was made very clear to her that you did not visit the grandparents without attending church, among other strict rules, such as not being able to eat anything without praying for thanks first. My grandfather would give his own sermons to the family every week, using the documents and biblical typologies that were in the family book. He would frequently attend church and take notes on the sermons given, returning home to add more content, and share the sermon with the rest of the family. By creating and adding to these documents in the family book, the same religious morals were carried over from generation to generation even after his death. There were cemeteries at both properties where family members were buried, used as recently as the 1980s, which assisted in preserving genealogical knowledge. The new land owners that purchased the property from our family were left to take care of these burial grounds for us.

In her childhood, my mother vividly remembers daffodils annually growing alongside the original farm cabin. Although the cabin is now gone due to change in ownership, the flowers still grow, indicating the location of the old house even after it was gone. Around the property is a large thorn vine that tended to take over the area if not tended to. Currently, the vine has grown over the family cemeteries, indicating that the cemeteries are no longer in use and are, unfortunately, neglected by the new owners. Seeing the area in disarray disappointed my mother, indicating that the practice and preservation of our tangible family heritage had been negatively affected by the change of ownership; however, the intangible memories of the area and use of the area will continue and passed down to future generations.

Modern Christianity in My Family

My family continues to practice Christianity and still considers it as the foundation of our family principles, morals, and values. Throughout my life, our Christian beliefs passed down from our Baptist ancestral background heavily influence our decisions in life such as employment and church participation. My immediate family, including myself, is very active in our Christian beliefs, thus paying tribute to and preserving our religious cultural heritage.

My mother grew up in the Baptist church, practicing the theology and practices that our ancestors of the Bush Settlement also practiced. My father; however, had a different theological background, growing up in the Presbyterian Church. When my mother and father married in 1988, my mother began to attend the Presbyterian Church. Although my mother no longer attended the Baptist Church of her ancestors, the Baptist theology she grew up with continued. My father attended Rogers Memorial Associate Reformed Presbyterian (ARP) Church since his birth, and was heavily active in the Church until 2009 at the age of 44. During these 44 years, my father had various roles in the Church. This included acting as the Business Administrator, actively participating in multiple ministries, holding several terms as a deacon, and being part of the worship band. He also served at various points as the director of the PointE (an evangelical interdenominational outreach ministry to middle and high school students), Cross PointE Kids (an outreach ministry for elementary school students), and RMC Children Summer Camps, among other ministries. My father also served as President of the Men's Club, went on mission trips to Mexico in 1982 and 2005, and was elected as a church elder. Although my parents religious backgrounds had some differences and occasionally caused disagreements on theology, my family continued to attend the Presbyterian Church for 21 years, until 2009. Throughout this time, my mother's Baptist beliefs challenged my father's Presbyterian background, leading to the family's conversion to the Baptist denomination.

In 2009, while my father was an elder of Rogers Memorial Associate Reformed Presbyterian Church, the disagreement on the topic of infant baptism between Presbyterian and Baptist beliefs encouraged my father's decision to leave. My mother's Baptist background led to the challenge of this theology, leaving my father to question the family's participation in the Presbyterian denomination. My mother's Baptist beliefs concluded that the dedication of infants was a covenant between the parents and church congregation to partner in raising the child in Christ, and not intended to decide the child's relationship with God. As the child grows up, his or her decision to be baptized becomes a personal choice. However, Presbyterian theology believes that the baptism of infants is necessary. Both denominations agree that baptism is an outward sign of inward change; however, the Baptist Church holds that an infant is incapable of inward change. Tensions between these two theologies led to the return of our family back to my mother's ancestral Baptist faith.

This began when a family of the congregation wished to dedicate their child to the church. This was a problem, because the ARP Church did not practice infant dedication, but infant baptism. This event prompted many discussions, meetings and led to research and brought into question the validity of infant baptism. Since my father was an elder of the church, he began to research scripture. From this learning, he then began to challenge Presbyterian theology, arguing that infants should not be baptized. My mother and her family's belief that baptism is a symbol of personal faith and public profession of this faith influenced his thinking. His question to the Presbyterian Church was, if baptism is the proof of the personal belief and acceptance of Christ into life, how could infants truly be baptized since their minds are not sufficiently cognizant to do this? He argued that babies are incapable of understanding religious beliefs, and thus cannot publicly declare their faith. This argument created tensions between him and the rest of the congregation, resulting in the church leadership seeking outside council.

The church brought in doctors of theology from Erskine Seminary to explain the Presbyterian theology of infant baptism. Discussion among the leaders led to the decision of the elimination of the practice of dedications, but instead the child would have to be baptized as an infant. The church also decided that only ordained ARP Pastors are permitted to perform baptism and have to be performed in the context of a worship service, meaning elders are incapable of performing baptisms. Unable to convince my father that this theology and practice of infant baptism was biblically based as the sole means of baptism, my father decided to resign from his positions and leave the Presbyterian Church for the Baptist Church. Incidentally, two other elders serving with him also had a change of heart regarding infant baptism. One resigned and one stayed.

After leaving the Presbyterian Church in 2009, my father began to work as the technical director of North Rock Hill Church, belonging to the Southern Baptist denomination, until 2013. Currently, the family attends a non-denominational church whose government and theology reflects southern Baptists beliefs with the inclusion of a contemporary style of worship. The preservation of my mother's Baptist religious heritage continued into her time at the Presbyterian Church and encouraged my father to research scripture, thus resulting in his change of theological belief regarding baptism. From that point forward, my family identifies themselves as Baptists, further continuing the beliefs of my maternal ancestors and preserving this religious cultural heritage.

Today, I am personally preserving the religious cultural heritage of my family by being an active member in Christianity. I have served on the leadership team of a nondenominational Christian organization at the College of Charleston, called Journey, for over three years, and am currently the organization's president. Through Journey I volunteered on a mission trip to Cuba in the spring of 2017. My participation in the Church and my beliefs in Christianity passed down to me from my parents directly reflect the importance of Christianity in my life. This reveals that the preservation of Baptist beliefs and values of my maternal ancestors have thus far been successful. From working on this research I have realized that I have not been baptized in the traditional way of the Baptist Church. Therefore, I find it necessary to make the personal decision to be baptized, continuing the religious legacy of my family and making a public declaration of faith. In challenging my parents on why I was baptized as an infant in the Associate Reformed Presbyterian Church, my mother explained that she knew that I would one day ask questions and at that time be able to come to my own conclusions of how my outward sign of inward change would take place, reminding me of what we learned from my father's experience in the Associate Reformed Presbyterian Church.

Religion remains a contemporary driving factor in family decision-making. Baptist beliefs passed down from my maternal ancestors of the Bush Settlement to my mother influenced the direction of our current family values. Our family's act of moving due to disagreement of religious theology is a similar situation of the migration of my ancestors from Virginia to Kentucky in 1784. The pattern of Baptist theology in my family and the power it holds on the decision of my family is a direct reflection of the life of my ancestors. Furthermore, the continuation of these belief practices preserves the intangible aspects of our religious cultural family heritage.

Conclusion

Religious cultural heritage is a form of preservation that encompasses the significance of houses of worship, community, and religious faith. This has been the driving force for my family ever since the establishment of the Bush Settlement in the late eighteenth century. For my family, the preservation of Christian morals, beliefs, and traditions are crucial to the understanding of our family, which has been maintained through careful recording keeping and the continue observance of our faith unto today. The Old Meeting House Church has undergone multiple physical changes over the years. According to the National Register for Historic Places nomination, "the upper windows on the sides were taken out and the center mid-level window lowered to the level of the bottom window.

At a later date the front entrance was moved to the opposite end of the church facing the cemetery. The rectangular windows were altered to the present narrow Gothic ones."[46] The location of the entrance has also been changed to the opposite southeast wall sometime before 1870. In 1949 the church's interior and original galleries were destroyed by a fire. However, later restorations restored the white interior, leaving only the gallery at the southeast end to be replaced.[47] By restoring the white church interior with local materials, the building continues to hold high integrity through its original use.

Although the Old Meeting House has been successfully preserved, it fails to accurately sustain its religious cultural heritage. The church does not participate in the practice of observing the intangible aspects of its history. There are no resources available to the public regarding the church's beliefs and practices throughout time; therefore, it failed to recognize the spirituality of the community throughout time. It has been suggested that the church members should begin to record its history, collect sermons, and document traditions practiced during meetings to ensure that religious intangible heritage is preserved for the future.

The work done in the preservation of religious heritage in my family has been very successful due to the act of keeping family records, oral histories, family research, and the continuation of traditions similar to those of our ancestors. The continuation of Christian faith in my family today is visible proof of the successful preservation of our religious heritage. Just as the passing down of these records and family history is important, so is the passing down of religion. To better preserve our religious cultural heritage, it is suggested that we continue collecting family vital records, such as dates of baptisms and detailed writings of our current beliefs and traditions. This will ensure that our current Christian faith can be carried over for future generations and analyzed without room for misinterpretation. For instance, my great-grandfather William Clayton Rutledge in explained his biblical typologies, located in the Family Book, that we would be able to better understand his thought process, intention, and morals of the time by what he wrote. Lacking this type of documentation, it leaves room for inaccurate analyses and discrepancy. Religious cultural heritage preservation is a growing theme in Christianity today. If done effectively, this type of preservation will not only preserve the fundamentals of Christian beliefs, but also preserve the traditions of families that prioritize religion.

Chapter 5: Living, Learning, and Loving: A Story About Family Heritage and Preservation

By Cara E. Quigley

For anyone that has ever taken the time to sit down and *really* look at a jigsaw puzzle, one would be able to tell you there is more to it than just a pretty picture to look at after countless frustrating hours spent trying to fit pieces together. Each individual piece contributes to the overall final product in a unique and special way. People have different strategies they choose to go about solving a puzzle. Some might look for commonalities, such as colors or patterns, whereas others put together all of the edge pieces first, forming an outline for the bigger picture to be filled in. By extension, each family tree is a puzzle made up of an assortment of pieces that in one way or another, are meant to fit together and form something beautiful. The parents, grandparents, children, uncles, aunts, cousins, friends, and even pets are the pieces that have a lasting impression on the larger whole.

For my senior thesis research project, I am focusing my research on family memory, the value of memories, and how they evolve over time, which serve as the pieces of the family history jigsaw puzzle portrait. Particularly as story pieces are passed down the line of a family, it is important to recognize what characteristics make each family unique in how they fit together. I began thinking about this a lot lately, most importantly because several of my relatives have developed Alzheimer's, dementia, or some other form of memory loss. Loss of memory is also sometimes symbolically represented as a fragmented jigsaw puzzle, which is another reason why this analogy is so befitting. I realized that through my research and writing on family heritage, having a collection of thoughts and memories that have been significant to my family is needed for our own preservation success. As many of my relative's memory continues to diminish, they can look back on this history that I have documented and, for at least a moment, be reminded of some meaningful moments from our family's past. They are the reason I am doing this scholarship: to honor their lives and to see to it that their memories live on. This is my gift to them.

I have structured this paper into several topical sections. The first section focuses on my personal experiences in my hometown of Galveston, Texas and the history of this place in general. I discuss how my interactions with Galveston have not only contributed to my overall family heritage, but connect myself and my relatives to others of the past. I then go on to focus my research on the Irish immigrant experience and their search for the American Dream. This family history is also contextualized in a short literature review pertaining to the value of memory. Lastly, I end this exploration with a conclusion, summarizing how all that I have found will serve as a memoir for my family. The research, time, effort, sweat, and tears I have dedicated to this paper represents one more piece set in the jigsaw puzzle portrait of my family's heritage.

A Saltwater Soul

Because of growing up on an island, I always felt a sense of comfort when I was near a body of water. The beach became more than just a place to build drip-sandcastles with my cousins, or get the perfect tan; it became part of my identity. I believed as long as I was close to the ocean, I could go anywhere I wanted. Beyond the shore of Galveston, Texas was a world of opportunities waiting for me to discover. From the time I was a toddler, I was essentially a walking advertisement for Coppertone Sunscreen on the beach. Everyone remembers the copper-tone baby with her diaper being pulled down by a puppy, exposing her tan lines. Yes, that was me as a kid. My cousins were always jealous because I *somehow* came out with an olive complexion rather than the fair skin the rest of my Irish family had. What can I say? I was lucky. However, my cousins did repeatedly try to convince me that I was adopted, but given my resemblance to my grandparents, that was *highly* unlikely.[1]

As I became older, I continued to have a unique bond with the ocean. I fished often with my dad, spent my fair share of time on the boat, and surfed frequently with my friends as I became older. When life hardships got the best of us, the beach was our safe place. For whatever reason, salt(water) in our wounds didn't hurt us, it healed us. It made us stronger because we could always rely on the ocean to complete and connect us. We simply had what the locals called a "Saltwater Soul." When I turned seventeen years old, I became heavily involved with Galveston Island Beach Patrol

(GIBP), an agency of the United States Lifesaving Association and designated lifeguard service for the City of Galveston. GIBP is a Texas Department of Health certified first response agency, employing over a hundred people composed of lifeguards, senior guards, supervisors, peace officers, and dispatchers. The mission of GIBP is to "protect the 5-7 million people who visit the Galveston beaches each year, respond to aquatic emergencies 24/7/365, educate the public about beach safety, and be a good community partner."[2]

Beach Patrol is a unique responsibility to handle, particularly for a young person. Guards are not only taught to protect beach patrons but to also be advocates for the ocean. We have seen firsthand the damage that can be done to a family if someone does not listen to the rules we enforce. Anyone can accidentally get sucked into a current and panic. To see the look in someone's eyes as they are beyond scared for their lives, swallowing mouthfuls of water and beginning to sink beneath the waves is something you can't get out of your head. The ocean is not a pool; it is a magnificent monster. Visiting families rely on us to protect them to that everyone makes it home safely at the end of the day. The water not only has the power to claim lives, but also to destroy cities. I always grew up having to deal with hurricane evacuations. Beach Patrol always was responsible for being front line soldiers in these natural disasters, so the influence of hurricanes was always very impactful on my life. It is because of my early childhood exposure to the ocean on Galveston's beaches that have instilled in me a special connection to this place's history.

Watching the waves roll down the coastline on my drive to school along the seawall eventually influenced my future decision of where to go to college, live as an adult, and raise my children.

When I made the monumental decision to leave Texas and attend the College of Charleston, in South Carolina, I was confident my past experiences prepared me for this journey. Reflecting on this particular point in my life caused me to connect myself to my family members who followed a similar path for their own, which eventually led me to where I am today. If it wasn't for the ocean, my ancestors could have never sailed from Ireland to the United States to start a new life. Whether or not we choose to follow the liquid road is a determinant of what we hope to see along the horizon for our future.

Tiny, but Mighty

Galveston is a barrier island located on the coast of Texas along the Gulf of Mexico. Given that I was born and raised here, I never truly appreciated how important the Island was until I moved away. Galveston is small, but mighty; for such a petite place, she has been through a lot over the years. Like the rest of North America, the island was first inhabited by Native American tribes. In 1528, Spanish explorers led by Cabeza de Vaca were shipwrecked on the sandy island, resulting in the first Europeans recorded as setting foot here. The men quickly discovered they were not alone, and encountered the Akokisa and Karankawa peoples. Cabeza de Vaca and his men lived among the Karankawa tribe for four years as captives.[3] It was not until Cabeza de Vaca became a skilled medicine man and diplomat that he won the respect of the Karankawa, and the small group of men were finally freed. While these Spanish explorers' first encounter with what became called Galveston island was accidental and rather unpleasant, it did inspire other explorers to seek other lands in the vicinity. This land would one day become Texas.[4] If it were not for these adventurous conquistadors searching for fame and fortune, who knows where my family would have eventually ended up. The discovery of my beloved Galveston sandbar is relevant to my personal heritage because not only did the Spanish stumble upon new lands for their king, but they established what would become the home to my family centuries later. It was more than a new territory; it was a new beginning.

Galveston island remained territory of the Akokisa and Karankawa for several hundred years more until it was finally visited by French Pirate, Jean Lafitte. He is the most famous known pirate to have ever called this island home. In 1812, Lafitte had traveled to Galveston after being forced to leave his home at Barataria Bay, near New Orleans. Although Lafitte was not harming any U.S. ships, the United States government required him to leave after causing tension with other countries. It was said that "Lafitte was known to prey upon Spanish and English vessels, thus creating antagonism between those two countries and the U.S. government for harboring such a fugitive pirate."[5] This community, Campeche, formally established by Lafitte in 1817 was used as his base, where he was actively raiding ships traveling through the

Gulf of Mexico. Even to this day in Galveston, specific names given by Cabeza de Vaca and Jean Lafitte are implemented in one way or another. For example, neighborhood communities I grew up in or ran around with friends in were named in reference to them, such as Campeche Cove, Lafitte's Cove, Pirates Beach, and the San Luis Pass, are just a few that were significant to my growing up in Galveston. After four years of continued privateering exploits, the United States had once again had enough of Lafitte's mischief. In 1821, he was ordered to leave Galveston island.

To leave a lasting impression upon vacating the United States., Lafitte burned the town to the ground after loading up his gold and escaping to Isla Mujeres, off the coast of the Yucatan.[6] It has been rumored that "his treasure is buried on Galveston Island or hidden up any of several rivers and streams around Galveston Bay. There are accounts of dredges occasionally coming up with gold or silver in the spoils as they work on the shipping lanes of Galveston Bay."[7] While I myself have never ventured into the yard and ruins of what was once his Maison Rouge, several treasure hunters have. Trespassing became such an issue on the site that in 1960, a chain link fence topped with barbed wire was erected in an effort to keep out hopeful diggers.

While stories of pirates and indians on the island have the sneaky suspicion of embodying Peter Pan's "Neverland," Galveston was a very prosperous location. The first permanent colonists arrived on the island in 1827 before finally establishing what is today Galveston in 1836.[8] This was the same year Texas became an independent republic from Mexico, marking this significant period in Texas history. When the city was incorporated in 1839, Galveston quickly became the most active port west of New Orleans and the leading port of Texas. “In 1842, Galveston received the first cotton press in Texas. By 1899 Galveston was the world's foremost cotton port and the fifth most important port in the United States.” [9] Galveston was also an alternative port of arrival for European immigrants coming to the United States, as part of an effort to settle people in the interior. With a population of 36,000 people, Galveston was the first city in Texas to have electric light, the first to have telephone service in the state, is home to the oldest medical college in Texas, and is where the first opera house in the state was founded.

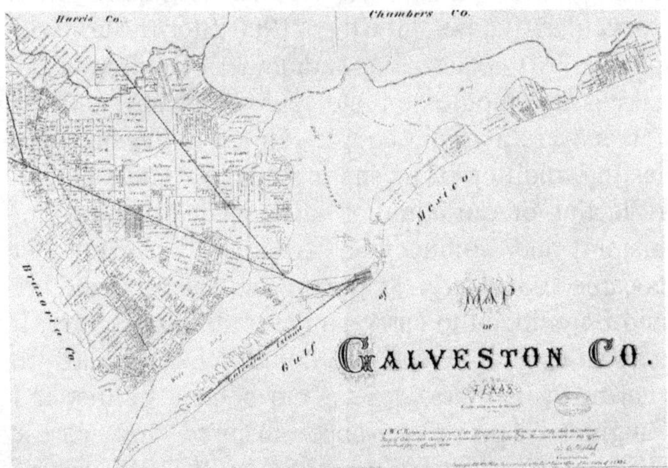

Figure 5.1: Map of Galveston County, Texas from 1879. Library of Congress Geography and Map Division.

My love for historic preservation began in Galveston when I was about eight years old. Every year on Mother's Day Weekend, my mother and I would go on the Galveston Historic Homes Tour put on by the Galveston Historical Foundation (GHF). The tour consisted of several, privately owned historic residences on the island that have been researched and opened to the public. The information presented to visitors consist of a specific family's journey to the United States, heirlooms they acquired overtime, their involvement on the island, etc. Mind you, this is not a house museum tour. The homes on the tour changed each year and it was always so exciting to see how the current residents maintained where they lived. My favorite pictures were of what the home looked once like when it was originally built, particularly those with the "1900 Storm Survivor" plaque. My paternal grandmother, Bobby, began taking my mother on the tour when she and my father were a young couple. This was the start of a lasting tradition of us sharing quality time together, reflecting on our common interests and passions for history and architecture. After my grandmother became too elderly to go on the tour, my mother and I continued to carry on the tradition together. It was a special event we could look forward to sharing every year, growing our bond as mother and daughter. This experience inspired my career aspirations in historic preservation. It is because of this exposure to history and architecture that I acquired a passion for preservation, which eventually led to me earning a degree in this field.

This first impression of historic preservation marked a turning point when I could place myself in the shoes of people from the past. I gained a better understanding of what life was like for them and had the opportunity to compare and connect my life to theirs. Another major connection was my shared experience with natural disasters. Galveston is positioned in a vulnerable geographical location along the Gulf of Mexico, where there is always a risk of severe weather. Throughout my twenty-two years living in the coastal cities of Texas and South Carolina, I have seen my fair share of hurricanes. However, none of these storms compare to the horrors endured by Galveston residents in 1900.

1900 Storm and Grade Raising

To this day no other natural disaster impact in the United States equates to the destruction of the 1900 Storm in Galveston, Texas. This significant occurrence was a wakeup call for the U.S. Weather Bureau. It was evidence that the Bureau needed to advance a more accurate form of communication if they intended to protect the American people from hurricanes.[10] The Galveston hurricane made people realize this was a situation where politics did not have a place.[11] Obviously, the ability to forecast severe weather has improved since this period in history. However, even if the forecast sent from Washington, D.C. had been accurate at the time of the Great Storm, how would tens of thousands of residents have been evacuated from the island in such a short period of time? Perhaps we will never know how many people could have been potentially saved from eminent death if the forecast had been on point, but we can learn from this tragedy.

In the early morning of September 8, 1900, the citizens of Galveston had no idea the horror they were about to endure. Lightening cracked so loud your eardrums would ring as it lit up the jet black sky. The wind roaring at a whopping 135 miles per hour tore through the city destroying more than 3,600 structures. Islanders were dragged from their homes into the demonic water contributing to a death toll ranging between 6,000 and 12,000 people.[12] This single natural disaster left the city devastated.[13] The port, being the main source of revenue for the island, was destroyed. Thousands of bodies washed up on shore or were discovered under piles of debris during storm recovery. Streets that had once featured beautiful grand homes were now heaps of rubble and splinters. Only a few lucky structures remained standing. Many islanders, who were lucky to be alive, were left homeless. Clouds of smoke from large cremation fires rose into the air, filled with the stench of burning flesh. It was said that Galveston would never fully recover.[14]

In an effort to protect what remained of the barrier island, the U.S. Army Corps of Engineers constructed a 17-foot seawall, along with a city-wide "grade raising." The jacking up of some two thousand surviving structures with hand-turned jackscrews — from shanties to a massive Catholic church — helped to bring this back community. The sand fill was dredged from the Galveston Harbor entrance and then transported to neighborhoods through a 20-foot deep, 200-foot wide, and 2.5 mile long canal with four self-loading hopper dredges.

Figure 5.2: An opened passageway in the debris, North on 19th Street, Galveston, Texas. Library of Congress Prints and Photographs Division.

Figure 5.3: Sea wall construction site, Galveston, Texas, c.1910. Library of Congress Prints and Photographs Division.

After the fill was discharged in the areas to be raised, new foundations were constructed on top of it."[15] Both the seawall and the grade-raising were regarded as engineering marvels of their day.[16] While this project was intended to shield the island from future storm damage, it additionally facilitated drainage and sewage systems.[17] The construction of the wall took place between 1903 and 1911, working in incremental quarter-mile square sections.[18] Since then, the island of Galveston has had the opportunity to rebuild, grow, and become an iconic, historic city. The lone-standing homes and businesses that somehow withstood the horrors of the 1900 storm are recognized in Galveston today with a special plaque. These can be seen scattered throughout the city, displaying how random and detrimental damage was on the island.

The surviving buildings symbolize the strength the island community embodies and the willingness to not give up when times are rough. From the survivors, we have the opportunity to learn from these tragedies that have occurred, appreciate what we have been given, and recognize the chance to start fresh once again. When the storm hit, there was no other option for the community other than to rebuild. When I was growing up in Galveston, hurricanes were common and it taught me so much about how to handle emergency situations. When I was in fifth grade, I was shipped off to Kentucky to live with my aunt for a short period of time while a hurricane swept by the island. The neighborhood was destroyed to the point that many of my friends were forced to move into temporary homes, rebuild completely, or move because of the damage. I was lucky to only have three feet of water in our garage so we only lost storage items. Many of my friends and their families did not return to the island because of the damage their homes received. This experience, though not as deadly as the 1900 storm, still allowed me to form a connection to those of the past who survived the great hurricane. We were still forced to rebuild the island and many people suffered drastically. Luckily, the surviving homes and businesses were a foundation to build from. Mother Nature tried to get rid of the island, but she did not succeed. After the 1900 storm, the remaining citizens of Galveston had something to go off of when they decided to rebuild. It was not an entirely blank canvas. For people immigrating to the United States, they did have to start from scratch in a new country. My family was one of these. The link from the families of the past to the present is what continues to serve as a bond for heritage and the state of its preservation.

Discovering A Common Thread of Simplicity

When I think about my family heritage and the state of its preservation, I think about the legacy I am leaving for future generations. I realize many of my morals and life experiences are a reflection of my past relatives that have been passed down over time. As discussed by the National Register of Historic Places, much of the direction for historical research is being referred to as the "new social history."[19] It is explained that "most historic places represent the everyday lives of ordinary people."[20] This is applicable to my family in more than one way. While the locations significant to my family are not nationally recognized as historic, they were important in the daily lives of my relatives. The bulletin goes on to say, "stories about people, the places they came from, the reasons they came, the lives they led, their work, their families, and their connections with other members of the community and with the outside world."[21] I have been told unbelievable stories revolving around my Irish Catholic roots, the crazy memories of relatives spread all over the country, and how our family came to be. I was lucky enough to come from a family where sitting around in a big circle and talking about our memories is a tradition. There may not be one monumental event in our history that defines my heritage, but the presence of small influential moments has been carved into our hearts and minds forever. It is the little things that matter, and it makes no difference if no family member is ever considered heroic to the rest of the world. What matters is that they were heroic to my individual heritage.

Until recently, I never considered how closely my family is connected to other families of the past who led common, simple lives. The majority of the population were the common people. As I have come to study historic preservation, my appreciation for the fun little tales of family traditions, and memorable moments has grown as I can see they are far more valuable than tales of how wealthy or powerful someone became. The stories of love, silliness, and character, rather than monumental acts of valor or greatness are what is important. In fact, it is said by the National Register, "where once historians pored over the papers of the political leaders of the nation's past, today they study building permits, census records, wills, diaries, deeds, and newspapers as well. They also pursue information not found in written records, such as oral histories and the material culture of everyday life."[22] This is extremely important to the transformation of how we view our history. If you don't know where your family has been, how do you know where to go? How do you want to be viewed in the future in comparison to the rest of your family? Every time my family sits around to tell stories about our relatives' lives, I learn something new and gain a modified perspective to life. As I've gotten older, I have been allowed to hear more controversial conversations, risky stories, and participate in discussions that are not suited for young people's ears. As I grow and mature, so does my appreciation and understanding of the jigsaw puzzle pieces that make up my family. What I have seen my relatives partake in has taught me much about love, value, and self-worth. We have worked hard to get to where we are now, and we have loved one another through and through. The most valuable inheritance my family can pass down is our love. This is a love that is full of quality time together, accepting of our flaws, and appreciating how fortunate we are to have so many memories to reflect upon. Traditions have been formed and passed down that connect people through time.

The decision to leave everything behind and start fresh in a new country can be both daunting and terrifying, yet exciting at the same time. What is a person trying to accomplish when they venture into the unknown or take a major risk? They are exhibiting a major character trait that the family name will carry throughout the rest of history. The hardships and the pain will be worth what they are sacrificing so that others can be happy. These are the monumental moments in my family heritage that greatly changed us. This is why it is important to remember our heritage and to encourage the preservation of your mark on history.

The Luck of the Irish

Galveston was a one of the main points of entry into the United States, along with Boston, New York, Philadelphia, and San Francisco. Immigrants came to this country in search of better opportunities than where they had come from. The chance to start fresh again and achieve the "American Dream" was very sought after, and this has not been very well documented in Galveston among the Irish. This was certainly the case for my father's family, when they came to the United States, and eventually moved to Texas.

When I had a chance to search through my family's history, it made great sense why I had such an astounding upbringing of Irish Catholic rooted traditions, customs, and viewpoints in all aspects of life. Whether having to do with religion, family and marital standpoints, politics, culinary tastes, or even our proclivity to burn when exposed to direct sunlight, the practices continued over generations in my family made me who I am today.

Both sides of my family are from Ireland. While it might be assumed each side of my heritage had a similar background story, what they each brought with them from their homeland, was different. Character defining elements range everywhere from physical features such as my dark brown hair and eyes, my religious and political views, how to best raise a family, and how to love and respect one another. All of these minuscule details are the explanations for what it truly means to be a member of my family. The annual gatherings each summer in Galveston with unbelievable tales of my uncles and aunts growing up in Texas influenced the way I want to raise a family in the future. This sort of influence in a person's upbringing is a derivative of the concept of social memory. More specifically, Robert Goodin and Charles Tilly explain that "individual memory is the dynamic medium for processing subjective experience and building up a social identity."[23] This is to say that the brain is subject to continuous development throughout regular social interactions and exchanges with significant individuals in our lives. They continue on to say, that "in the shape of stories and anecdotes transmitted in oral communication, some of the episodic memories can transcend the individual person's lifespan. They are recycled within a period of 80-100 years, which is the period within which the generations of a family- three as a rule, but sometimes up to five- exist simultaneously, forming a community of shared experience, stories, and memories."[24] This explains why we continue to retell or recycle family memories. As they are orally repeated over and again, passed down through generations, they are being recorded repeatedly in the cognitive file drawer of memories. In the case of my family, our ritualistic story telling sessions late at night do just as social memory states it does. It ties us together and will continue for generations to come. I was lucky to have this sort of social interaction with my family's Irish heritage.

The Fighting Irish: The Quigley Family

My great-great-great grandfather, James Gratton Quigley, was born about 1858 in Ballymote, County Sligo, Ireland. He was married to Mary Ferriter McCarthy in Ireland. James was involved with the Ireland Republican Army, which was primarily active in the protest of the British Empire's control of Northern Ireland. This struggle against colonization began during the 1500s. Because "the settlements were called Plantations. They 'planted' Protestant settlers in Ulster who were loyal to the British monarch. The rest of Ireland remained Catholic and generally opposed to British rule."[25] The Irish were focused on independence from the British. It was common for violence to break out in small scale rebellions during the 1830s, 1840s and 1860s. "Most of these rebellions were organized and led by the Irish Republican Brotherhood. They were usually known as Fenians, after a mythical Irish army in the past."[26] This primarily was what my great-grandfather was involved in. Considering that James was very active in the protest, he was disliked by the monarchy. He stood strong in his opinions of freedom and would do anything to be loyal to Ireland.

Nevertheless, by "the 1880s, Irish resistance to British rule was becoming more effective, mainly because it was using democratic methods. The Irish

Home Rule Party campaigned for Home Rule for Ireland. This meant Ireland would still be part of the British empire, but it would have its own Parliament. The vast majority of Irish Catholics supported Home Rule - they thought an Irish Parliament would treat them better than a Parliament based in London."[27] This is where things become tricky. There now was division among the Irish people in how they wanted to control their homeland.

Many opinions continued to float around but the main concern was who was going to run the new Home Rule Parliament? Would it be the local people, or would they be brought in from Great Britain? In terms of local wealth and power, "a number of wealthy Protestant landlords also supported Home Rule. They thought that they would be running Ireland's new Home Rule Parliament."[28] So, in the 1880s and 1890s the Parliament in London voted on whether to give Home Rule to Ireland. Both times the measure was rejected for two main reasons:

1) There were a large number of people in Ireland who wanted to keep the Union between Britain and Ireland. Most of these Unionists lived in Ulster; and
2) Many British MPs felt that if Ireland got Home Rule then the rest of the British Empire would fall apart.

If they gave Ireland Home Rule, why should they not give India Home Rule too? The British government managed to ignore the Home Rule issue until the early 1900s.[29] As a result of this, there continued to be riots and protests on who would have authority. Many rebels, such as my great-great-great-grandfather continued to speak and fight for what they thought was right for the country; however, the situation grew out of hand.

James was now a wanted criminal for committing crimes against the British government from acts of protest. In efforts to escape prosecution, James and Mary immigrated to the United States. Their point of entry was through Boston. Since James was on the run from the government, there was no formal documentation of their entrance into the United States.[30] However, we do know it was in 1876 thanks to Quigley family records. When Mary McCarthy, my great-great-great grandmother, came over with her husband James, she brought with her one trunk. This trunk included all of her worldly possessions. Scratched onto the rusty lid on the trunk was her name and the destination "Boston." This trunk is now a family heirloom and was given to my Aunt Joan by her grandmother. On the inside trunk lid, a note from Helen Murray Quigley, December 18, 1966, reads:

> Joan, your Great-Great Grandmother, Mary McCarthy, who was my Grandmother, brought this trunk from Ireland when she came to live in Boston, Mass- 1876. It was given to me by my mother, Ellen Theresa McCarthy Murray, after a few years. It was given to me about 30 years ago.[31]

This trunk serves as a monument for the family. Since James and Mary entered illegally, this was important documentation of our family's initial journey to the United States. While they were running away from Ireland to the United States, with hopes of starting fresh and building a life,

James joined the police force in Boston right off the bat. My grandmother used to say, "he ran to the U.S and was on the force the next day."[32] I'm not sure how accurate that "next day" time frame is, but we do know it was a quick transition. James and Mary were among many Irishmen who entered Boston at this time period. Since the Potato Famine taking place in Ireland in the 1840s, Boston's population has radically changed.[33] It was said by "1875, sixty thousand foreign-born Irish were living in Boston. During the balance of the century immigration from the poverty stricken island continued so rapidly that despite the growth of the city the Irish newcomers and their children made up from 30 to 40 percent of Boston's total population."[34] The influence of the many immigrants coming into Massachusetts greatly changed the character of the city. This could be seen by the cultural practices and traditions brought by immigrants from their homelands.

While in the United States, the Quigley's had five children. The first of the Quigley children born as a legal American citizen was my great-great grandfather, Bartholomew Sarsfield Quigley on May 1, 1892 in Milton, Norfolk, Massachusetts. The remaining four Quigley children born to Mary and James came into the world between 1892 and 1897.[35] In 1917, when Bartholomew was twenty-five years old, he was drafted into the World War I. His draft card described him as being of medium height and build, with brown hair and blue eyes.[36] But he claimed exemption from the draft as he was the main support for his mother. His listed occupation was as "Claim Adjuster" for the Massachusetts Employees Insurance Association, located at 185 Devonshire Street, Boston. This was a mutual company created by the Massachusetts Workmen's Compensation Act. [37] In 1921, Bartholomew married Helen Murray in Milton, Massachusetts.[38] Bartholomew and Helen remain in Massachusetts for a short while before relocating to Illinois. While residing here, the couple welcomed a son into the world, my grandfather.

In Chicago, Illinois on January 27, 1929, James "Quig" Sarsfield Quigley was born to Helen and Bartholomew Quigley. He was the only child the couple had. Quig graduated from Loyola Academy in 1945 before heading to the University of Notre Dame for his bachelor's degree, which he completed in 1950. James then continued his education at Notre Dame University Law School, receiving his JD in 1951. While in law school, Quig became best friends with a fellow classmate, George "Edwin" Pletcher, from Perryton, Texas. Edwin was one of seven children from a farm family in the Texas panhandle. At the time of this new friendship, Edwin's little sister, Barbara "Bobby" Inez Pletcher, began attending St. Mary's Nursing School in Notre Dame, Indiana.[39] With her big brother keeping a watchful eye on her every move, it was no surprise that Bobby and Quig would soon become acquainted. With her dark, curly hair, creamy white skin, petite frame, large entrancing brown eyes, and moist red lips framing a slightly crooked grin, Quig was smitten.[40] It would not take long for her to become irresistible to him. When he first invited her on a date, nobody had any idea this was going to be the beginning of a love story right out of a movie.[41]

While Bobby and Quig were engaged, they exchanged letters back and forth between Illinois and Texas while he was working in Chicago and she was living at home in Perryton. Anyone who reads even a few lines of their correspondence can tell right off the bat how smitten these two were for each other. During their time apart, they would express their love, update the other on the events of their day, teasing one another with silly pet names or inside jokes. You simply cannot read their words without cracking a smile. My favorite letter was written by Bobby the week before their wedding. The note was still in the original envelope, mailed from Texas to Illinois with her flawless, dainty script spelling out my grandfather's name and address. I can only imagine the joy that overcame him as the envelope was dropped on his desk by the office mail boy. Eager to see what his future bride had to say, he ripped the side of the envelope, which had the label "via airmail" stamped across the top in purple block letters, to pull out two crisp sheets of paper. They are covered front and back with words written in blue ink, swirling gracefully across the pages. Her words are genuine as she writes,

> ...a week from now we'll be together. Darling, I can hardly believe it, that at long last our dreams will come true. I want you to know that no matter where we go or what we do or what may happen to us, I love you, and my every prayer is that I'll be as good a wife as is possible and will make you happier than you've ever dreamed of being. -- God bless you, sweetheart. I love you forever. -- your Bobby"[42]

The paper has lingering scents of sweet perfume, and tobacco as Bobby's father, George, sat in the living room smoking his pipe while she wrote the letter. The morning of October 25, 1952 in Perryton, Texas, Bobby woke up early after tossing and turning the night away. She couldn't help but be overcome with excitement to begin her last day as a Pletcher girl. Later that afternoon, she would forever become Barbara Inez Pletcher Quigley, and she could not have been any happier. While getting dressed for her big day, Bobby's white bridal gown reflected the sunlight as it shone in through her childhood bedroom window. The light creeping in glimmered against the sheer fabric that elegantly covered her chest, perfectly matching the sparkle in her eyes. Her arms wrapped in lace sleeves would soon be wrapped around Quig forever. As she pulled her long veil over her head, covering the bonnet placed atop her head like a tiara, she studied her reflection in the mirror one last time. When she arrived at the church and stood at the beginning of the aisle, her father offered his arm out to escort his daughter to her groom. Waiting at the altar was a tall young man, dapperly dressed in a dark suit with a patterned tie and a carnation pinned to his lapel. Nervously fidgeting with his blue Notre Dame class ring, he beamed up at the lady dressed in white walking towards him. He couldn't take his eyes off her and knew at that moment; this was only the beginning of a magnificent journey with the woman he loved so deeply.[43]

Bobby and Quig became husband and wife on October 25, 1952 in Spearman, Texas. On that day, Quig presented Bobby with a 14 karat gold wedding band. Engraved on the inside of the ring reads their initials and wedding date, "J.S.Q. - B.I.P. 10-25-52" to commemorate this joyous union. Their rings symbolized more to them than just a man and woman following societal norms. Their rings symbolized an eternal life of love, support, and companionship as they enter this next phase of their lives. The hole in the middle of the rings resembles a void that has been missing from the other person's heart. Through the act of the other person wearing this ring as a symbol of the unending love and affection, the void is now being filled. Nowadays, Bobby's wedding band is a family heirloom. By recognizing the love these two had for one another, we can continue to expose the rest of our family to the same passion they had for one another. We can learn by example of how to create a good life for our family. Upon my grandmother's death this past October 2019, I was given her wedding band to keep her and my grandfather close to my heart. Wearing a piece of jewelry that is as significant as this does so much more than remember those loved ones we have lost. Heirlooms, such as this ring, are souvenirs from a family's journey down a windy road. They are key accessories to the identities and relationships created along the way, which led to where one's cultural heritage is today. This ring was a key feature of a monumental life experience that marked the entrance to many more life milestones, altering life as a family knew it.

Shortly after their marriage and honeymoon, Bobby discovered herself to be pregnant with their first child. Upon returning from their newly wed travels, Quig was asked to serve in the U.S. Army during the Korean War in the Far East Command. While he was away, he and Bobby continued to write each other letters every day.[44] Quig discusses his travels in Korea, the beautiful landscapes and how he wished he could share it with Bobby. When Quig had finished his time in the service, he was honorably discharged and sent back home to join his family in Chicago. He was finally able to officially begin his law career as a trial attorney in his dad's law office.[45] The reunion of Bobby and Quig was the first time they had gotten the chance to live together, and now they found themselves with a third roommate! They welcomed their oldest daughter, Joan Therese Quigley, in 1954.[46]

From that point on, Bobby and Quig were never without children in the house. Their small little family grew from three to eight in a matter of years. After Joan came Mary Margaret "Peg", Bartholomew "Bart", Patrick, Kathleen, and Daniel "Danny."[47] By the time the rest of the children began to arrive, Bobby and Quig decided to move their family from Chicago to Houston, Texas. While in Houston, Quig became the Vice President and Chief Claims Attorney for the Pan American Cos. A later purchase by Anderson Clayton led to his Vice Presidency and Chief Claims Attorney for The Ranger Insurance Cos.[48] Given that Houston was not more than an hour away from Galveston, the Quigleys frequently visited to escape the busy city. They decided to build a beach house on Bermuda Beach, on the west end of the island. Bobby and Quig planned for this beach house to be where they retired. Every day, they looked forward to when they could finally sit on the porch together, listening to waves crash on the shoreline with pelicans flying across the cotton candy sky.

Quig built this house for his family with his own two hands, a heart full of love, and a dream of a future with the love of his life. He built it as a place to foster a new life for our family, once his children had grown up and moved away. This was where he could watch his grandchildren play in the sand, splash in the waves, and make memories that would last forever. This dream Quig created is the link which connects my family to those of the past. The families who traveled to the United States, whether it was legal or not, were in search of something. Perhaps they were looking for a new beginning. A dream where they have taken risks so their grandchildren could have a wonderful life. While it may not seem like the construction of a beach house is a representation of a significant moment in history, it was for Bobby and Quig. From the moment the pilings were set, a new era of family traditions was on the horizon. Over the next few years, Quigley and Pletcher family memories would take place within the walls of the house.

Some years later, my dad and Uncle Bart built another house next door to the Quigley beach house. They lived here together until my dad bought Barts half from him. When my parents got married in November 2, 1991, they began their small family in this house. When I arrived six years later, this is the home I was raised in.[49] It is because of my grandparents experiences that led me to where I am today. If they had not built a beach house in Galveston, my family would not have established themselves there, allowing me to be a real island girl. The beach house is where my earliest memories take place, sitting in a circle with my cousins, staying up late on the deck having long talks with my relatives. This is where influential moments took place and with the people who contributed to the Quigley family heritage.

Hungry for Luck: The Hughes Family

I was regularly exposed to family members on my father's side of the family, but many of my mother's side of the family had passed away by the time I was born or at least old enough to realize the significance of our interactions. Keeping this in mind, my main experiences with my mom's side of the family was told to me rather than remembering it on my own. To make things more cohesive, a full family record of my mother's heritage was created to help me position myself as a randomly assorted puzzle piece in this mixed up world. In this case, the Hughes family is a puzzle all its own.

The name Hughes is one of the top 50 most common surnames in Ireland.[50] It has been said that the Hughes family name (O'hAodha in Gaelic), and is descended from the mythical King Milesius, who lived c.1600 B.C.E.[51] Another story suggests "the founder of our branch was Cormac Cas, who in turn was the son of the King of Munster about the year 148 C.E. Suffice to say the family goes back a long way."[52] The name "Aodh," from which Hughes derives, represents the descendants of fire. This is one of the deities or gods that was worshipped by the Celts in pre-Christian times.[53] Given that any sort of relation to a favorable god was a very popular claim to fame, many families continued to hold onto the given name in the times following the events of St. Patrick and the conversion to Christianity in the country. When the English ruled over Ireland, they insisted on translating the original Gaelic names into English. In efforts to anglicize the name "Aodh", it was translated to Hugh. As a result, many surnames were changed as well as family links because of this. The O'Neills in the north (who later on became the Earls of Tyronne), became Hugh O'Neill, before becoming Hughes. The decline of the Gaelic-Irish language continued to occur between 1650 and 1800, as many people living in Tyronne began to only speak English with Gaelic as a far second, less common language.[54]

As far as religious practices are concerned within the Hughes family, there is not one individual who is more influential than Archbishop John Hughes (1797-1864). Bishop Hughes's family immigrated to the United States when he was twenty years old from Tyronne. Following a short time period after arriving, John entered the seminary.[55] Despite his initial feelings of the Church not being active enough in the support of Irish nationalism, he set those opinions aside devoting his life and career to the Church.[56] While in the United States, Bishop Hughes made his way from immigrant clergy, to being Archbishop of New York, all the way up to the builder of St. Patrick's Cathedral and the prime influencer of the modern American Catholic school system.[57] Since many Irishmen came to the United States with little educational background, it was important to Hughes to create opportunities for his people so they could also seek the American Dream.

Figure 5.4: The Right Reverend John Hughes, D.D., coadjutor & administrator of the Diocese of New York. Lithograph by J. Penniman, c.1840. Library of Congress Prints and Photographs Division.

It was said that "Hughes's view was that education was the surest way out of poverty. No Catholic prelate was more vocal on that subject, and no one was a more aggressive fundraiser for the cause. Build the school before the church, if you have to, he told his priests. More and better schools, more and better teachers, would reduce the crime rate, make the Irish more employable, and allow Catholic Irish-Americans to live a more economically stable, spiritually grounded life."[58]

Bishop Hughes also acted as an emissary for President Abraham Lincoln during the Civil War, and was heavily active in the support of Irish nationalism. It was said that "no man ever exercised a deeper or wider influence on the Catholic Church and the Catholic mind in the United States" than Bishop Hughes.[59] While he was only a very distant cousin, he is still one of our own. His spiritual values and traditions that he spoke so passionately about have been passed down through each generation of our family, Bishop Hughes is a role model American and honored Irishman, as demonstrated through the loyalty and faithfulness to his people and his God. This has been taught to me since I was young and I will continue to pass these teachings down to my children.

Bishop Hughes and his influential role in the Catholic Church, much of the remaining family in the Ireland traveled from Tyrone to Belfast, before later sailing across the Irish Sea to Glasgow in the western Scotland Lowlands. When the Irish Potato famine struck, it hit small Irish holdings hard. Nineteenth century Ireland was in bad shape as farms were becoming smaller, crop prices were dropping, and fertility rates were continuing to increase."[60] The economic change was drastic and certainly caught my family in the middle of its wake. At this time, my great-great-great grandfather Charles "Charley" Hughs was 22 and his wife Ann Sweeny was 19. I find this situation particularly relatable considering the current crisis the United States is in today. With the hardships being endured with Covid-19, our economy will suffer significantly, millions of people are falling victim to the virus, and it is creating a "new normal" for our lives. I am currently the same age as Charley was during the famine, so I have a better perspective on how he must have felt at this time of hardship.

The Potato Famine was a turning point in Irish culture and the Arthur Wellesley, the Duke of Wellington, noted that "there never was a country where poverty exists such as in Ireland today."[61] Thankfully, the mining industry began to take off as greater demand for pig iron and other ores created a new influx of jobs and economic expansion. This opportunity allowed Charley to make a living for his family as he and Ann brought ten children into the world. Mining continued to be a line of work for my family for many years. In addition to the Hughes were the Mother-ways. This side of the family was headed by Robert, as he emigrated to the United States after surviving the great famine.[62]

When Robert left Ireland, he was a single man in his early thirties. Like so many other immigrants coming from impoverished homelands, Roger could neither read nor write when he arrived in the United States.[63] It was up to him to learn so he could find well-paying employment. He eventually became literate, but was never able to fully master his writing skills.[64] While living in New England, Roger met Mary O'Brien. They were married in Hartford, Connecticut in 1852 and together, they had six children, but with only three surviving. Now that Roger had literacy skills, he was taken more seriously and found work with a railroad company.[65] Thanks to this opportunity, Roger was able to establish himself in an industry and feed his family. Roger's initiative to problem solve, in order to build a better life for him and his family, shows future generations how meaningful our relatives' paths are to our personal heritage.

Conclusion

It has been said that when someone you love becomes a memory, that memory becomes a treasure. It is these treasures that continue to keep our family alive. It is incredibly important to continue to pass stories, traditions, and morals through the family tree so that they will not be forgotten. Those who were once the true embodiment of what it meant to be a good spouse, parent, aunt, uncle, cousin, or friend will someday be gone. What they leave behind is a legacy. The hearts they touched and minds they molded are what truly matter in the preservation of our heritage. We can continue to share experiences that will influence us for years to come by living, learning, and loving one another.

On October 26, 2019, my grandmother, Bobby, passed away. The day before she died would have been her and Quig's 67th wedding anniversary. We all believe she suffered from heartache after being without her loving husband for nine long years. She wanted to be with him again, and now they could be. Her funeral was one of the hardest days that I have had in a long time, but at the same time it gave the family peace of mind. She and Quig had made their contribution to our family heritage by providing us with many skills and lessons to carry all throughout our lives. The path that they took together, combining knowledge from different experiences or solving problems, culminated in her contributions to our family. She and Quig were living proof of what an idyllic, long lasting love and marriage looks like. They showed us by example that with love, good communication, and putting God and family first, you can be successful.[66] The research I have collected for this project is a unique contribution to the overall topic of social memory, proving how valuable memories are to the preservation of family heritage. This paper is also significant to the subject of social memory, as I have portrayed how present day lives, traditions, and morals are mirrored from the past. Prior to this, no formal documentation or memoir had been written for my family in an effort to make sense of the value of our memories. This project serves my family as a collection of thoughts, feelings, and acts as well as a steppingstone for the future progress of our heritage.

Our family jigsaw puzzle is still continuing to be worked on, making the overall picture clearer each day. By understanding the motivations and hopes of our relatives who came before us, we can learn how their aspirations and goals are reflected in ourselves. A great deal of time and effort has been sacrificed in order for us to be standing where we are today. It is because of what these people were able to accomplish that led us to become the additional puzzle pieces we are meant to contribute to the family portrait. Connecting our modern day selves to those of the past will underscore the importance of creating family memories together, and preserving our heritage for others to come.

Chapter 6: Pluznik Stories About the Holocaust

By Rachel Pluznik

Every Friday night growing up I remember looking out the window and seeing the sky turn shades of orange and blue, followed by my mom yelling for my brother and I to come to the dining room. I would walk into the amber-yellow dining room and see my dad, mom, brother, and our dog sitting by the bar-top, in front of our weekly Friday night layout. My mom, being the only woman of age, would start lighting the heavily tarnished, silver candlesticks in front of her while chanting a blessing. Then it was my dad's turn, to take the similarly tarnished, silver wine cup and say his prayer and then pass the puckering sweet Manischewitz wine to the rest of the family. The last job was my brother and my responsibility. We would pick up the freshly warmed loaf of crusty Challah bread and say our prayer, eagerly awaiting our chance to rip off a piece of the perfectly baked manna that filled our nostrils of yeast, salt, and honey. I loved this tradition because it not only connected me to my parents, but my parents to their parents (and so on), as well as millions of other Jews around the globe, spanning thousands of years.

My dad is an Israeli who moved to the United States when he was only twelve years of age. He has one older brother, Meir Pluznik, and they have a mom and dad who are divorced and both remarried. Being an Israeli plays a huge role in the identity for everyone on my dad's side, yet I did not know much beyond that. I knew the names of my dad's brother, aunts, uncles, and my grandparents, but I really only knew them as abstractly related to me. A huge part of my family history is that my dad's extended family was impacted by the Holocaust (1941-1945). The horrible things that happened in concentration camps and the Holocaust in general have been explored by society and scholars in great depth. Although an overview of the events that became the Holocaust is very important knowledge for everyone in my family, the personal story of those like my grandfather who escaped the concentration camps are very important too, and not as often shared and remembered. My grandmother also has a completely different experience than my grandfather. As she is younger than my grandfather, she did not witness the Holocaust, but her parents and brothers did. Stories like hers have also not been shared to the extent that they need to be. Being Jewish is a huge part of my identity, yet somehow, I have lived until now without knowing much of my family's experience.

Through preserving my grandparent's histories; I will analyze the different experiences Jews of varying backgrounds had in relation to the Holocaust. Many people of my generation do not have direct, first-hand accounts of their family's Holocaust experiences. Many people who were alive during the Holocaust and have descendants my age, either died during the Holocaust or have passed on since. The generation that witnessed the genocide and survived are not sharing their stories because it is hard to talk about or difficult to remember their stories properly because of age. The number if living survivors is also diminishing through time, as they age. Compared to other students or millennials that have researched and written pieces reviewing similar topics, this will be a comprehensive examination of almost all the different experiences that Jews in my family had throughout the Holocaust, as well as direct experience from other people. Unlike previous studies such as *Life and Loss in the Shadow of the Holocaust: A Jewish Family's Untold Story,* by Rebecca Boehling and Uta Larkey and *A World Erased: A Grandson's Search for His Family's Holocaust Secrets*, by Noah Lederman, I will use my family as an example of how memory of the Holocaust still shapes Jewish lives today. I want to preserve these stories of struggle and perseverance that shaped my life and the Jewish people. This paper is about my family's life in relation to the Holocaust and Judaism in general. This paper will serve not only as a way for me to get closer to my heritage, but also serve as a preservation tool for others of my generation who may not have access to their families' history to utilize and learn from. Whether my story helps others preserve their own stories or is used to provide a more personal, critical outline of the events and effects of the Holocaust overall, it will help educate and assist in preventing genocide like this for future generations.

Road Map to This Paper

In order to successfully accomplish my goals, there are a few things that need to be discussed before going into my family's history. Learning about some of the events and details that make up the Holocaust allow for a better understand of why the stories of individuals who experienced it are important. After talking about the ghettos, concentration camps, and Night of Broken Glass, this is when my story will be introduced. Since there were so many outcomes for people after this horrible time, it is easiest to start with a story of someone who was one of the lucky few who could live to tell their tale, Joe Engle. His story articulates the brutality and awfulness of life in concentration camps. This is part of the Holocaust that my family did not experience, but under different circumstances could have just as easily have been them. From there, my paternal grandmother's, Nechama Pluznik, story begins. Both my father, Daniel Pluznik's parents and grandparents were impacted by the Holocaust. Nechama Pluznik, or "Safta" as I call her (meaning grandmother in Hebrew), was born after her family had already escaped Vienna, but luckily her parents were able to tell her their tale so she could write it down. From her story I transition to my grandfather's story. His family was also from Vienna, but escaped later than my grandmother's family did, before ghettoization but after the Night of Broken Glass.

My paternal grandfather has since passed away, but luckily his brother, Michael, who lives in Israel was able to give me an insight into their family's struggles. Lastly, there is a case study of a twenty-year-old girl, Anna Katz-Stiefel, who had a fatal end, which was the most common outcomes of the Holocaust for those who experienced it. She has one of the most important stories to share even though she is not related to me. By suffering the fate that most Jews experienced during the Holocaust it is crucial to share Anna's story with mine especially considering that I am of her age when she died at the writing of this paper.

Preservation is not just about the past but also the present and future. That is why my family heritage story does not end with my grandparents. The Holocaust was an event that would change people and continues to change people for generations to come. I began this research by talking to my dad and uncle who were born in the first generation after the Holocaust. I am the current (and likely last) generation in my family that has direct access to the personal experience in this historic event. What my ancestors had to go through shapes how I am able to live today and will likely influence those descendants to come if they are educated about it.

Overview of Events that Shaped My Heritage

"Holocaust" is Greek for "sacrifice by fire," and that is exactly what the Nazi mass genocide of six million Jews and other persecuted minorities was.[1] It began as simply the Germans excluding Jews from economic, political, and social parts of society, as well as encouraging them to leave Germany. The Nazi regime targeted all that were too different from their vision of the superior race. This spanned from homosexual Germans, Gypsies, Jews, and people of different political backgrounds, such as the Communists.

One of the first events that marked the beginning of the Holocaust was "Kristallnacht", better known as the Night of Broken Glass. This event is important because it was the last chance Jews had for fleeing the Germans. Kristallnacht is important because this is the night that my grandfather and his family chose to flee. Kristallnacht occurred from November 9-10, 1938. It was the night that the German Nazis made it known that they wanted the Jews to die. The Nazis stormed cities in Austria and Germany that night and attacked anything that was related to Jews: people, businesses, houses, synagogues etc. It became known as the Night of Broken Glass because there were shards of glass that lay over the entirety of the streets that night. The violence continued into the day of November 10. Police were instructed to arrest the Jews that dared to interfere, instead of helping them. In the span of two days over a thousand synagogues were damaged or destroyed, 7,500 businesses were ransacked, and 30,000 Jews were arrested.[2] This night marked a crucial date in the start of the Holocaust and World War II. After this, people had an inkling of the horrors that were to come and that this hatred and brutality from Hitler was not going to blow over.

As World War II progressed so did the German's means of purifying Germany of Jews. They forced Jews into ghettos as the first step. The ghettos were usually the worst, run-down, dangerous areas of the city. Not only were Jews forced to leave their homes with little notice, but they could only bring with them what they could carry. Once arriving in the ghettos, life did not normalize for these displaced people, it only got worse. The Jews received minimal food, minimal space, and few freedoms. Overcrowding got so bad that the spread of diseases such as tuberculosis and typhus was a constant threat. Things only became more terrible from there as Jews from small towns were brought into the same city ghettos. Due to the conditions of the ghettos and nearby slave labor camps over half a million Jews suffered and died. The Germans, who coined the term *Lebensraum*, took the meaning to a whole new level. *Lebensraum*, meaning "living space", was a belief that German's thought to be imperative for their survival. In Hitler's *Mein Kampf*, he declared that Russia would be his target for *lebensraum*.

The original purpose of a concentration camp, being forced labor, was maintained intact throughout the progression and growth of camps around Europe. However other punishments and torture tactics developed as well. Within the camps, prisoners were ranked based on reason for incarceration and how useful they were within the camps. If they were elderly, children, or women they were often considered not useful, or ranked very low, so they were often sent to die in the gas chambers or shot on the spot. Whereas, if they were a young adult or middle-aged male, they were considered of higher value and would be sent to work at the labor camps. That is until they would undoubtedly fall ill or injured and be considered not useful. [3] Of course, the ranking system was not always so black and white. The future of someone was not always decided by the Nazi soldiers organizing them. Sometimes, if they were incredibly lucky, someone who was feebler would escape certain death and live to tell the story.

Joe Engle: In Insight to the Minority Outcome

My paternal grandfather, Dov Pluznik luckily never had to experience the concentration camps and my paternal Grandmother Nechama grew up in Israel years later. Although their stories are the ones that are most directly related to my heritage, it is crucial to compare their stories with others who had similar origins, but different endings to fully understand the Holocaust. Joe Engle, one of the few remaining Holocaust survivors in Charleston, South Carolina, had a story more similar to my grandmother's parents. Both my paternal grandmother and grandfather's family escaped before Hitler, but the only record we have of them is through the stories that my grandmother has told, and pictures she and my grandfather have saved. Joe Engle's story, although a minority in the outcomes of the Holocaust, still plays an integral role in filling in gaps in my history that my family did not experience.

Engle was born in Poland, near Warsaw and was the eighth of nine children. Growing up in a country that was anti-Semitic was an introduction to what the rest of his years in Europe would be like. Even before the war started, he remembered that every Jewish person had to wear a yellow Star of David on the outside of their clothes in order to be identified as Jewish. Engle witnessed fifteen people being killed on the spot to spark fear for being Jewish. At the beginning of the war, he and his family moved into the Warsaw ghetto with some of their things. This was after Warsaw had been bombed, so not only did they have to leave their home, but they had no new home to go to due to the bombing. The ghetto was six blocks large with a fence and guards preventing anyone from leaving. It was as if the free Jewish people had turned into rabid dogs and been rounded up by guards to keep in a shelter, unable to harm the rest of society. Joe had witnessed this harshness in his young age, but little did he know this was just the beginning.

Figure 6.1: Section of eight-foot high concrete wall encircling Jewish ghetto in Warsaw, Poland, 1940. Library of Congress Prints and Photographs Division.

Joe was fourteen and a half when the Nazis ripped him from his parents and siblings and put him on the cattle car. He left his parents for the last time and began what seemed like an endless, horrifying train ride that ended with an even more horrid destination. He "was in it, and [he] was by [himself]." [4] Joe was unloaded into his first internment camp, entering a gate with a sign that read "if you work hard enough, you might survive [arbeit macht frei]."[5] That is the moment he knew that his experience was only going to worsen and he was not sure if he was going to make it. He recalls the camps being very poorly built. Made out of wood, but not very sturdy, as if they were built in a hurry and made to change locations. When he arrived, he said you would "lose your hair and clothes. They gave you numbers and striped uniforms to wear."[6]

Figure 6.2: View of German concentration camp at time of liberation by U.S. Army, 1945. Library of Congress Prints and Photographs Division.

At this point, Joe was no longer a person, but a prisoner with a number. His meals consisted of a piece of bread and margarine for breakfast, a small cup of "soup" (mostly water with a few floating bits of potato here and there), and then a cup of coffee with a slice of bread and margarine again for dinner. The Nazis determined that prisoners could survive off of sixty calories a day, so that is what they did. Joe recalls that through all of the horrible things that were happening, he remembered that there were musicians, the best he had heard, who would play music. It was such a contrast in senses. Being so down, undernourished, overworked, and then hearing beautiful melodies filling the air of such an awful place. After spending some time at Birkenau, he remembered soldiers coming and asking for volunteers to go somewhere else. In his head nothing could be worse than what he had been experiencing at Birkenau, but he was wrong. They put him on a train to Auschwitz, where he soon learned that what he had experienced before was nothing in comparison to what he was about to live through. He went to a work camp where he learned to lay bricks. Luckily, he was able to work, so he buried himself in it. The worst part of his recollection was that of the sensation you have when you smell someone incinerated from the crematorium. "Everyone wanted to live, but everyone thought of death."[7] He did not see an end to this torture, but he knew he wanted to survive.

His story starts to take a turn for the better at this point. Prior to the arrival of the Russian Red Army, the Germans started to move the prisoners west. This movement was known as the death march. He, and hundreds of others, were herded into a stadium and sat overnight waiting for a train to pick them up and take them to Germany. Once again, he was loaded into a train car like a sardine, except this one, unlike the other, had no roof. This was his chance. He said, "I've got nothing to lose. If I stay, I'm not going to make it anyhow."[8] So he jumped from the moving train car into a pile of snow. He buried himself there until the soldiers determined they were never going to find him. He was seventeen years old at this point, in the woods of Czechoslovakia with nowhere to go. He eventually found his way to a farm where he got lucky enough to meet a man that would introduce him to the resistance. Joe went on to train with the resistance and fight back against the Nazis as a partisan. He was involved in the bombing of a German Police station and countless other dangerous attacks. He did not care about the danger, nor did anyone else he was fighting with. While he put his life at risk, he was happy to do it as long as he knew that he was doing something that would assist the defeat of the Germans.[9]

The last step of Joe Engle's story is the story of his liberation. Joe was liberated by the Soviet Red Army in 1945. He was ready to leave the resistance at this point because he had done his fighting, but he realized that there was a point that if he kept going, he would be just as bad as the Nazis and he "wouldn't stoop so low as the Germans." This is when he had to make the choice about "where to now"? He first chose to go back to his hometown. After this, he decided to go to the American Zone and ended up in Charleston, South Carolina. Once he arrived in Charleston, he met a group that helped him figure out that he had family that had also found their way to South Carolina. Three of his brothers and one of his sisters had also survived the concentration camps, and coincidentally decided to come to America and settle in Charleston. He started to rebuild his life back again. He got an American haircut and opened a dry cleaning business, Glamour Cleaners. [10] Engel's new life was better, but he will never forget the years that were taken from him, reminiscing, "I lost my youth and I lost my education".[11] He will always remember what he lost, but he swore that since he survived, he would tell his story "over, and over, and over, and over again".[12]

Engel is still alive today and telling his story. He embraces his past, the good, the bad, the ugly. "I am a Holocaust Survivor" is a tag he wears every day, with the dates and his serial number from the camps. People are invited to ask him questions. His story is being preserved through his relatives and Charleston's Holocaust Memorial. Every time his nephew, Michael Engel, looks at his "84009" serial number tattoo, it reminds him of his Joe Engel's experience. If Joe Engel sees someone walk through daffodils it reminds him that "the Desert will bloom with flowers, that's like me, I bloom."[13] Although Joe Engel's story is a rarity, it shows that Holocaust survivors can be resilient and will keep fight for what is right.

Joe Engel's story, although very different from that of my ancestors, helps fill in the gaps to what my ancestor's lives could have been had they not been lucky enough to escape when they did. It easily could have been my great-grandparents that got sent to a camp and were separated from each other and experience the torture that Joe endured. My family history would not be as important without his story as a counterpoint. When thinking about the Holocaust, it is important to remember that *everyone* was affected. Whether they went to concentration camps or were lucky enough to escape through hiding, it is when you learn about these stories together that you better understand why it is important to preserve Holocaust history.

Waskoutzer: Remembering Those who Escaped

My grandmother, Nechama, and her family are an example of those who were lucky enough to flee before Hitler sent everyone to the ghettos and concentration camps. Her great grandparents were Nachman and Jetti. They had five children: two sons and three daughters. On her mother's side, she had two aunts: Bini and Frances. This side of the family was also from Austria. My grandmother's parents had met because they had lived in the same apartment building. Her mother "would go to violin classes and [my grandfather] would pay Bini to tell him when to go so he could go with her and carry the violin." [14] My grandmother's first brother, Joshua, was born sixteen years before her, and the middle brother, Asher, eight years before her. Life was amazing for my grandmother's family, even though they did not have a lot of money. They were happy that is, until Hitler came to power.

Nechama's (my grandmother) parents, Jacob and Rachel, fled to British Palestine. Her father, Jacob, grew up as part of the Zionist movement, so he had the biggest connection to the Holy Land. Her eldest brother, Joshua was thirteen, the age someone under different circumstances would be having a bar mitzvah, and Asher was only four. My grandmother's immediate family is the most detailed story of my family and their relation to Holocaust that I have available to me. When they fled to British Palestine my great-grandfather, Jacob, got a certificate to take out money that he would get once arriving in their new home. He gave a detailed list of everything that he owned to the Nazis and got the money withdrawal approved. [15]That is just the beginning of a long winding story. In March 1938, when the Nazis arrived in Vienna, they were cheered on and praised by the majority of the Austrian people. During this time, Jacob was at work in his lumber yard that was located in the back lot, behind a candy shop. The woman who owned the candy shop had a house with a lot of land in the back, which she would rent out to my great-grandfather, Jacob. "He was there when my [great-grandmother] got a call from her friend telling her to tell my father not to come home from work because the Nazis were coming to get him."[16] As soon as my great-grandmother, Rachel hung up the phone, she immediately contacted her husband.

My great-grandfather was lucky to have the woman who owned the property his lumber yard was on, to hide him in her house and protect him from the Nazis. His landlord was nicer than most people were to Jews at this time. When the Nazis came to her house, she said "there are no Jews here." The Nazis, of course, still searched my great-grandmother's house anyway. The Nazis knocked on the door while my great-grandfather was in hiding, leaving just Rachel and her two children at the time, home alone. My grandmother's middle brother was only four years old when this happened, so he started crying from the men in the house, so the Nazis had enough and said, "let's leave these ugly Jews."[17] The next day Jacob returned home, assuming it was safe, but he was wrong. The Nazis came back and took my great-grandfather to "wash the streets next to the house with other Jews to humiliate them… brush the ground on their knees. This is when he knew that it was time to leave."[18] They packed everything they could fit in boxes to send to British Palestine, then got on a train to their first destination, Italy. Everyone else on the train were Jews that had also had the same idea to escape.

Between 1938 and 1940, over 110,000 Jews fled Austria. On the border of Italy and Austria my grandmother's dad took a top hat and walking stick and threw it out of the train, and said, "I don't want anything to do with them or that country anymore."[19] They spent a few days in Italy, and from there boarded a ship to Tel Aviv, after which they were dropped on the beach with little boats. My grandmother noted how this was very weird because there were no ports in Tel Aviv. They arrived on the beach on Shabbat, walked to a hotel, and asked permission to come in. My family had very little money at this time, but they assured the hotel that my great-grandfather Jacob was going to receive $1,000 that he had arranged to be sent to Jerusalem. He was an honest man and people trusted him. The hotel believed him that he would get him the money and let them stay. "He went on Sunday in a fully armored car to Jerusalem but could only get two-hundred and fifty dollars of the one thousand that he was promised, the rest they would give to him later."[20] He used this to live in the hotel for a few weeks. He and the rest of my grandmother's family then moved to a house on Yeula Street in Tel Aviv and lived there for half a year. They then moved to Trumpeldor Street. They still did not have enough money to buy a place, so they rented a room on the first floor of their building that my great-grandmother would sell furniture out of to make extra money. They only had to pay two lira a month for her room; a starting place for their dream of creating furniture. She did this for six months.

My great-grandparents always worked together, no matter what they were doing. Eventually they made enough money to buy a piece of land in 1950 that Jacob wanted to use to build a furniture factory on. He built half of the factory when he first purchased the land, but then ran out of money and could not finish it until later on when he could start making a profit. It was around this time when he got an affidavit from his brother-in-law to go to America and buy machinery for his factory. It all went as planned, until on the way back to Israel, his suitcase got stolen in Paris. My grandmother said that he came home and cried. "The machinery came after being transported on the ocean for several months and they were rusty and he had to throw most of them away because they would no longer work."[21] Only one machine out of all them worked, but the rest he had to throw away from rust. So, what did he do? He went to Germany to try and find new machines and was "lucky enough to meet a gentile who helped him buy machines. Thanks to him the factory started working. Imagine how many times they had to start all over again… but they did it."[22]

My Safta, meaning grandmother in Hebrew, was born in 1943, four years after her family fled to Israel. She grew up with a "normal" childhood compared to her two older brothers. Her dad had established a successful factory by the time she was a young child. They mass produce chairs and tables for military and hospital uses. A lot of her stories revolve around her mother and father's business. She remembered her father delivering products in a green delivery truck he owned. Her father was always the one dealing with customers, while her mother was in the factory with the workers. Nechama would sit in the back of the factory while her parents were working, smelling the wood shavings that filled her nose with every breath, and she would do her homework while she waited for them. Even though my grandmother was not personally affected by the Holocaust first-hand, she was reminded of it every day, not only by her family's experience, but by the other people she grew up around. In the home she grew up in, neighbors and friends had their Holocaust numbers stamped on their forearm, a permanent and painful reminder. It is those people that taught my grandmother how to speak Yiddish.[23]

By the time my grandmother was sixteen, her parents could afford to buy their first apartment of their own. This apartment would stay in the family for a long time, with my dad and uncle being born there. Recently, my grandmother had the chance to visit the building she spent her childhood in. She said "you always want to go back to where you were born. It was the place my father would come home from work whistling and I would run to the porch like he was my savior."[24]It is amazing to me that even though my grandmother and her family went through so much, they were able to overcome such adversity. As put perfectly by my grandmother, "those who are not resilient cannot survive."[25] This story is incredibly important to not only me, but to every Jewish person in the world. It is a reminder that even if the Holocaust was not during our lifetime, it stays with us still. It also reminds us that we, as Jews, are branches that come from a tree grown from the strongest roots. No matter what we as individuals, or as a religious group go through, we can survive, and this is an idea that everyone should be reminded of daily.

Dov and Michael (Miki) Pluznik: A Story of Those Who Escaped Kristallnacht

My father's other side of the family had a similar story as his mother's side with many parallels. My grandfather's mother was born in Eizenstat, Austria, near Vienna. His father, Meir Max Pluznik, was born in 1901 in a small town called Stopnica. This was a city in Poland that was part of the Austrian-Hungarian Empire at the time. He had eleven other brothers and sisters growing up. My grandfather's father, along with one of his brothers, left Poland at the end of World War I, and went with one of his brothers named Neftali, to Vienna. Luckily for them, since Poland was part of the Austrian-Hungarian Empire, they were allowed to move. Another brother of theirs, Petahia, had already lived in Austria when they left to move there, so they were able to meet up with him. Together, the three brothers opened a shoe factory that they called "Progress Shoes." They were able to start this company by purchasing surplus military shoes from the United States and using them to recreate shoes in Austria. Unlike many others during the time, they were very successful with their business. It was during the peak of their business when Hitler came to power, with about 200,000 Jews residing in Austria. That number was soon to take a drastic decline.

After my grandfather's father moved to Vienna, he met my grandmother's parents, Jacob and Rachel. While the two families had known of each other while in Austria, little did they know though that their two worlds would be so intertwined. It was also once my grandfather's father moved to Austria, that he met his wife, Melanie Pollack. "They got married in the beginning of the thirties, and their financial situation was good."[26] A few years later, my grandfather Dov Herbert Pluznik was born on November 7, 1935 in Vienna. His younger brother, Michael Pluznik was born eight years later on March 9, 1943 in British Palestine.

While in Vienna, both of Dov's parents were part of a Zionist organization in Vienna. When the Nazis came to power, the whole organization realized that they needed to get organized and escape to British Palestine. In 1938, in what was called the Anschluss, Nazi Germany took over Austria. For a short while "they were able to purchase a visa for businesspeople to go to British Palestine and were even able to send their furniture"[27] to meet them there. It was not until a year later that Dov and his family were able to get out of Vienna to go to British Palestine. On March 15, 1939, a few months after the Night of Broken Glass, my grandfather's family made plans to escape through Switzerland, to get to British Palestine; along with shipping their furniture and money out of Vienna. Thus, the family was able to restart a new shoe factory in British Palestine.

My grandfather's father and his two brothers that were lucky enough to make it to British Palestine, were able to escape the brutality that was to become the fate of so many in their hometown. According to my father's uncle, "in essence the Holocaust did not really affect my parents directly, however whoever stayed behind in Poland or Austria ended up getting killed in the concentration camps.[28] One brother and one sister got out and went to British Palestine, and two or three other siblings escaped and went to Brazil, but the others were part of the genocide.

Even though my grandfather and his parents did not personally experience the horrors of the Holocaust, they still lost much. According to Dov's brother, Michael, growing up "in our home we did not speak about the Holocaust, we grew up as Israeli kids completely. We got a European education. However, in the home we spoke German."[29] The first time he ever recalls his parents speaking about the Holocaust was after the trial of Adolf Eichmann in 1961. Eichmann was a Nazi leader during the Holocaust. He was presumed to be dead until he was "apprehended in Argentina in May 1960."[30] Once he was captured, he was tried in

Israel for his crimes against the Jews during the Holocaust. "He was known to have been an architect of the Nazi genocide and was even once reported to have said that he gained 'extraordinary satisfaction' from knowing that he had millions of death on his conscience." [31] During his trial he argued that he himself had never killed anyone, that he was just being loyal and obeying his leader, Hitler. From the time he was apprehended to the time his trial had ended, two years had passed. He was found guilty and was executed by hanging in 1962. His body was then burned as he had cremated the Jews in the Holocaust, and his ashes were then dumped at sea. This story stood out to my family because Israel does not have a death penalty and cremation is against Jewish beliefs, so for them to not only hang Eichmann, but burn him too, it got the attention of everyone, including my family. This is the only record of capital punishment in modern Israel. This trial, as horrible as it was, was enough to jump start the conversation about the Holocaust and become the starting point for information that would have otherwise been lost to my family.

My grandfather and his brother lived a normal Israeli childhood in the fledging new state of Israel. When they were children, Israel was under the British Mandate and there were British soldiers patrolling in Tel Aviv, but only until Israel's independence. His brother remembers Dov and himself growing up with a very positive view of religion. They would go to synagogue on Saturdays and on holidays, which is a tradition that they would pass on to their kids. "Everything was under the feeling of being free in our country."[32] People were allowed to be proud of their religion and feel safe in their homes and in their country, which is a luxury that their parents did not have. They followed religion growing up, but they behaved as they wanted to. My father's uncle, Michael, was the only one of his family born in Israel. As someone being born there, he "grew up with the chutzpah of the sabra."[33] Sabra is Hebrew for cactus fruit, sweet and soft on the inside but prickly on the outside. It is a moniker for the new generation born like Miki. He, along with my grandfather, served in the Israeli military when they turned eighteen. This is something that is mandatory, to this day, of every person with Israeli citizenship, but it is also something that everyone enjoys and is proud to do.

Dov served in the air force and tried to become a pilot but became a navigator instead. He also served during his reserve years as a part of the Israeli Military Intelligence Services, or as it is known in Israel "Aman". Once Dov got married to Nechama and had my father and uncle, Daniel and Meir, his life became focused around his career. He obtained his Ph.D. in Microbiology and Immunology, teaching at Bar Ilan University, and eventually become Chair of the Department of Microbiology. Dov discovered an important blood component that became the basis of many modern cancer treatment. He went on to become the president of the International Society of Experimental Hematology too. My father's family emigrated to the United states in 1980 during a sabbatical in which my grandfather was a visiting professor at George Washington University. He later worked at the National Institutes of Health and the Food and Drug administration. Working at NIH in Maryland was the reason for their move to the United States. He has sadly since passed, but his brother is still alive and well in Tel Aviv. His brother, Miki, went on to have a successful career in advertising and had two children and four grandchildren still living in Israel.

Figure 6.3: Dov Pluznik (Left), Melanie Pluznik (Middle Left), Michael (Miki) Pluznik (Middle Right), Meir Max Pluznik (Right). Photograph in the personal collection of the author.

Out of every story told, my grandfather's and his brothers are some of the best examples of how the Holocaust can shape life up until the present. Preserving their stories and the those of their parents and grandparents is evidence of how the Holocaust affects different generations. Their stories also are very relatable for anyone whose family may have come from similar backgrounds but were not able to live to tell about it. Their story is one that shows all of the negatives of the

Holocaust, family members dying and being forced from their homes, but also shows how resilient Jews are. Without sharing and preserving their side of the story, and how it shaped their life afterwards, that information and insight into their personal lives would have died with them. Sharing these stories means that those who died in the concentration camps, like my great-grandfather's siblings, or escaped like he had and created a new life of freedom, ensures their legacies will carry on.

Anna Katz-Stiefel: An Experience of One Who Died Young

Anna Katz- Stiefel was born on October 11, 1921 to Bertha and Isaak Katz-Stiefel in the village of Rauschenberg, Germany.[34] Her story is a very integral part of my family story, even though we are not related, because of the parallels between our lives. On August 27, 1941 she moved to Marburg, Germany. From there, on December 8, 1941 she was deported to the Riga Ghetto, which is where her story ends.[35] She was only twenty years old when she was murdered. She was almost one year younger than I am now when her life ended.

Not many details are known about her life in the ghetto, but there is information about what life in general was like there. Riga was the capital of Latvia and was home to around 50,000 Jews before World War II. When the Germans took over, they killed almost all the Jews that lived in the city, leaving only 4,000 survivors.[36] The mass murder was just a glimpse into what the life and more death in the ghetto was going to look like. From the few that survived along with the Jews transported from other countries, the Riga Ghetto was made. Some formed resistance groups and tried to escape, but Anna's story did not have a happy ending.

Although we know little of Anna's life in the ghetto, the Nazis who killed her have since been found, giving the world an insight into their actions, and specifically the moments before Anna and thousands of others in her same shoes died. In a newspaper article from the early 2000s, decades after the event, it had been noted that two men, Konrads Kalejs and Karlis Ozols, who had been two of the officers involved in the Nazi Death Squad in Latvia, were found and finally prosecuted for their crimes. In 1941, the 25,000 Jews of the recreated ghetto were marched to their death in a small forest on the outskirts of Riga.[37] It was only recently determined that Anna had been part of the Riga mass murder that was mentioned above. This massacre was just one of the many that stood out to the people prosecuting the two Nazi soldiers as being one of the most gruesome and awful. The officers that had been arrested bragged that "they'd used 25,000 bullets at Rumbula, [the massacre at Riga]."[38] One of the few survivors of the Riga ghetto, a man named Margers Vestermanis, worked as a slave laborer in the ghetto and recalls the pits the Nazis had forced them to dig. They were told they were for them, but he responded, "No. They're not for us, they're for you!"[39] He was sadly very wrong. On November 30, 1941, Jews were rounded up from the ghetto and ushered toward the mass graves they had dug for themselves. They were told they were being sent to another camp, however "many were aware they were doomed."[40] Once arriving at the soon to be mass grave, they were told to undress and "put one shoe in one pile, [the other shoe in another], clothing in another pile, driven to the edges of these mass graves."[41] Each person was then shot in the head, "one bullet per person."[42]

Today, people walk by the site where this tragedy occurred and what they all see is a litter of car dealerships and a small plaque of what happened. Few remember the lives that were lost in the forest outside of Riga. It is lives like Anna's that were lost, which is another reason for this paper. She is the reason that these stories need to be remembered. In a different time, that could have been anyone's fate, even mine, mass murdered in an unmarked grave without experiencing a full life. Because Anna's story is so personal to me, even though she was not part of my family's experience. I hope that through preserving her story along with my own, that people can feel the same way that I do when I hear her it and others like hers. People can read this and remember how lucky they are and feel connected to those who were not as fortunate.

Meir and Daniel Pluznik: The Next Generation

My family left Israel in 1980, when my dad was eleven and my uncle nearly seventeen. Sadly, my grandfather did not share his experience verbally with his children. Much like many other survivors, it is too painful of an experience to reminisce about. Everything that they know about him and his family's experience in relation to the Holocaust is told from my grandmother, his brother, or left in the notes and pictures that he has left us.

My uncle Meir, only recently met his cousins, my grandfather's surviving brother Neftali's children.

Growing up, Meir never met my grandfather's family. His childhood memories involve beach trips in Tel Aviv and weekly Shabbat dinners, but none involve my grandfather's side of the family. Since not much was shared with Meir about my grandfather's specific experience, it is important to look at what traditions my grandparents passed down from their childhoods, even if they did not verbalize why they were important. Given that neither of my grandparents grew up Orthodox, it is interesting to examine why my uncle and father did. Meir recalls "being dragged to synagogue every weekend… and having Shabbat dinner every Friday.[43] Judaism played a huge role in his life, even though the religious aspects did not seem enjoyable to him. Moving to America, Meir (Memi) was sixteen. He spent most of his early life in Israel, so the transition to America was harder for him than for my father. He describes his heart as always belonging in Israel. "My shell is Americanos, but my heart is Tel Aviv."[44] He has a deep-rooted connection to being Israeli yet says he does not consciously feel as if the Holocaust has impacted his daily life. As he has gotten older, he has found himself missing Israel more often. I asked if moving to America changed his view of Judaism. He put this modern view of Judaism and the Holocaust in different words. He said he became "more secular, becoming more academic than spiritual. The world had changed and [his] views changed too, but [h]e does keep Jewish tradition...you can't break 5,000 years of tradition."[45] Even though he may not notice that the Holocaust has impacted him, this is a modern example of how it has. The Holocaust has shaped his entire world and without those events he would not feel the deep-rooted connection to his past there. It is those traditions that he has passed on to his kids, such as bar and bat mitzvahs, Chanukah with his family, synagogue on the holidays, which my grandparents thought were important enough to continue to pass down through the generations.

As for my dad, Daniel Pluznik, he has a different view of Judaism, the Holocaust, and his life in Israel versus his life in America. Born August 11, 1969, Daniel Pluznik shares a lot of the same happy memories as my uncle, going to the beach and having family dinners, but he has a different view on Judaism. Compared to my uncle who is less religious but feels his heart is Israeli, my dad is more religious but feels his heart is American. Due to the fact that my uncle was deaf, their father had a very hard time relating to him, so he spent a lot of time with my dad. Meir could not go to synagogue with my grandfather on Saturdays because he could not hear the prayers, and it was hard for him to say them, so my dad went. My dad even learned to enjoy it. Apart from going to synagogue and having Shabbat dinner every Friday, my dad does not recall growing up very religious. He said that "in Israel they were observant, they had Shabbat dinner and attended services at the synagogue on the Sabbath, but then went to the beach with Safta after."[46] It was not until they moved to America that they became more observant. He never remembers my grandfather talking about the Holocaust, but looking back on his childhood, he believes it was those experiences that shaped the way he was raised. It seems as though his parents wanted them to grow up as children, something they did not get to do.

It was easy for my dad to recall all of his happy memories growing up, but harder for the bad ones. When asked what the worst childhood memory was, it was not as clear as some of his other, happier memories. He recalled a traumatic event in 1973, during the Yom Kippur War in Israel. It was normal to hear air raid sirens blaring when he was growing up. He even remembers people painting the headlights of their cars blue so the city would be a less visible target to an enemy bomber aircraft at night. It was one specific night he recalled that the air raid alarm was not a drill. He was four at the time and the air raid siren went off in the city "in the middle of the night and my dad was not home. We had a bomb shelter in the building where we lived, but the door was locked and someone had to break it down." [47] He remembers not being scared, but watching his mom try to tie his shoe and her being unable to because "her hands were shaking too much." He imagined the look she had was a similar fear as her parents had when the Nazis raided Vienna. The next morning, emerging from the bomb shelter where all the people from their building huddled in, he expected to see destruction. He even looked up anxiously expecting to see missiles in the air. Sadly, wars were a big part of life in Israel at the time, being a young country surrounded by enemies set on its destruction. However, when he emerged and looked up "it was a sunny day, a normal day."[48]

Figure 6.4: Daniel Pluznik age 13 (right) and his grandfather, Jacob (left) at the Western Wall in Jerusalem. Daniel, twelve, and Jacob are seen wearing Kippa, Tallit and Tefillin, reading from the Torah at Daniel's Bar Mitzvah. Photograph in the personal collection of the author.

My father and his family moved to the United States on July 4, 1980. They originally moved here with the plan of staying two years, as my grandfather was here for work, but they kept extending until they finally made the decision to stay. Daniel did not speak much English when the family moved, but learned most of it from watching TV. He went to public school for one year, but then transferred to a Jewish Day School, where my grandmother would eventually end up teaching too. He said that in Israel you did not have to try to maintain your Jewish identity as hard as you did in the United States. That is why when they moved to America, my father went to Jewish Day School. After moving to America, Daniel continued to go to synagogue throughout his childhood. Their house in the United States had a kosher kitchen, never mixing meat and cheese. To this day he kisses the mezuzah every time he leaves the house.

Through listening to both my father's and my uncle's stories, it becomes evidently clear that the Holocaust shapes every future generation, even if they do not realize it in the moment. It was my grandparents and their parents going through what they did that my father and uncle were able to grow up enjoying what it means to be Jewish, even if it was in their own ways. It was their struggles that allowed the worst memory of my dad's to be only when he was four. My father and uncle sat on the same beach every Saturday that my grandmother's parents landed on when they escaped from Vienna.

Rachel Pluznik: How do These Stories Shape My Identity as a Jewish Woman?

The question that remains is "what does Judaism and life after the Holocaust mean to me?" This is a very loaded question that has changed answers and continues to evolve over time. Growing up, my family belonged to a Jewish Conservative synagogue, but were not very observant of all of the Jewish Laws. However, there were key elements of Judaism that I carry with me today. Since my dad grew up Orthodox and my mom grew up Conservative, my childhood was a bit of both. We would keep kosher, with separate plates for meat and dairy. We never ate pork or shellfish, and we celebrated every holiday, including Shabbat every Friday. As I have matured, I have been able to determine what Judaism means to me, and how I want to practice it in my present and future life. Now that I am in college, I acknowledge every holiday and celebrate them in my own ways, but do not keep kosher or go to synagogue. My mom, dad, and grandmother still wish me "Shabbat Shalom" every Friday at dusk, and I dream of the soft, warm, perfectly sweet loaf of challah bread that I would eat as a child. In the future, I hope to bring back the traditions that I grew up with, such as hunting for matzah my parents hid on Passover and drinking Manischewitz wine with my kids.

I remember one time when I was around seven years old, I made myself an everything bagel with feta cheese smeared on top. I was so proud of myself until I heard my mom say, "Is that the meat plate you are eating on Rachel?" Instead of grabbing the white plate with brown decorations to the right of the oven that we use for dairy, I grabbed the one with black decorations to the left. My mom threw out my bagel out and then took me outside to bury the plate that I had used in the backyard because I had ruined the plate. I remember kissing the mezuzah every time I would leave the house and praying that I would be protected wherever I was going. I would also say the Sh-ma, the ubiquitous prayer Jews have recited for millennium, at bedtime. Out of all of these memories, the most important one to me is break-fast after Yom Kippur. Following a long day of fasting and being on edge, my entire family would get together and we would eat the biggest meal I could imagine. With a spread of bagels, souffles, sandwiches, and my grandma's famous chocolate-coffee cake, we would all break our fasts as a family. It was the moment we were all content and appreciative of what we had, both in terms of food and in terms of family.

Even though my family did not have many physical items from before or after the Holocaust to pass down, we had so much more. All of these traditions, from fasting, to eating traditional Jewish foods like kugel, to lighting Shabbat candles, are the things that I hope to pass down to my kids like my parents did for me. Especially after doing research on my family and learning what had been passed down, and how lucky we were to be able to hold on to so much during and after the holocaust, I know I will always hold my Jewish faith close to my heart. Now, when I walk by the Holocaust Memorial in Marion Square in downtown Charleston, South Carolina, I will remember every story I have learned about and the resilience of the Jewish people as a whole. As my grandmother tells me "Hitler tried to exterminate all the Jews in Europe, but you are a living example of his failure. Never forget your roots, and your future life as a Jewish woman." [49] The Holocaust is one of the worst genocides to happen in our world's history and should be remembered and preserved by everyone. Hopefully this paper and others like it will help the world acknowledge how the Holocaust impacts even our most recent generation of Jews.

Conclusion

Throughout the events of the Holocaust, my family lost their homes in Austria, their children, their siblings, their livelihoods, and their sense of safety. A lot of things that people of different backgrounds have been able to preserve through generations, my family and families like mine, were not able to preserve. There are no family houses, china sets, or family business that have been left for me or future generations. Instead, we preserve our traditions and our stories. Whether it be taking a sip of the overly sweet Manischewitz wine on Shabbat, or shredding potatoes to make my grandfather's famous latke recipe on Chanukah, I carry on the traditions that my ancestors grew up with. The story of my paternal side of the family is one that is important to not only me, but will eventually be so for my children and grandchildren.

Holocaust memories that I was fortunate to have access to are important because they show how far the Jewish people have come and if anything catastrophic were to happen again, that we could survive. For those without access to their own family stories, or even my children who will not have access to great-grandparents survivors, they now have a connection to their past and can learn what I directly received from my grandparents. Hopefully these stories will not only be a tool for those looking to document their own history, but also a reminder and warning for everyone else to prevent anything like this from happening again.

Endnotes

Endnotes for Introduction

[1] Barry L. Stiefel, ed. *What is Your Heritage and the State of its Preservation?, Volume 3: Putting Theory into Practice* (Berwyn Heights, MD: Heritage Books, Inc., 2018).

[2] Barry L. Stiefel, "Beyond Names and Dates on a Tree: How Librarians Can Help Explore Family Heritage and Preservation," *Genealogy and the Librarian: Perspectives on Research, Instruction, Outreach and Management,* Carol Smallwood and Vera Gubnitskaia, eds. (Jefferson, NC: McFarland, 2018), 156-63.

[3] Barry L. Stiefel, "'The Places My Granddad Built': Using Popular Interest in Genealogy as a Pedagogical Segue for Historic Preservation," in *Human Centered Built Environment Heritage Preservation: Theory and Evidence-Based Practice*, Jeremy C. Wells and Barry L. Stiefel, eds. (New York: Routledge, 2018), 289-308.

Endnotes for Chapter 1

[1] See Walter J. Fraser, Jr. *Charleston! Charleston!: The History of a Southern City* (Columbia: University of South Carolina Press, 1989).

[2] Melvin H. Jackson, *Privateers in Charleston: 1793-1796* (Washington: Smithsonian Institution Press, 1969).

[3] W. Chris Phelps, *Charlestonians in War: The Charleston Battalion,* (Gretna: Pelican Publishing Company, 2004).

[4] Donald M. Williams, *Shamrocks and Pluff Mud: A Glimpse of the Irish in the Southern City of Charleston, South Carolina* (Self-published 2005).

[5] Jean-Francois Theric in Melvin H. Jackson, *Privateers in Charleston: 1793-1796* (Washington: Smithsonian Institution Press, 1969), 120.

[6] Jonathan R. Dull, *The French Navy and the Seven Years War* (Lincoln: University of Nebraska Press, 2005), 243.

[7] P.M. Jones, *The French Revolution 1787-1804* (London: Routledge 2017), 33.

[8] Dull, *The French Navy and the Seven Years War*, 245.

[9] Dull, *The French Navy and the Seven Years War*, 254.

[10] Jones, *The French Revolution 1787-1804*, 31.

[11] William Doyle, *The French Revolution: A Very Short Introduction* (Oxford: Oxford University Press, 2001), 37.
[12] Doyle, *The French Revolution*, 40.
[13] Doyle, *The French Revolution*, 38-58.
[14] Mege, "Notice to the French and American Citizens, republicans, and my brothers," *City Gazette,* 17 August 1795.
[15] Mege, "Notice to the French and American Citizens, republicans, and my brothers," *City Gazette,* 17 August 1795.
[16] Jackson, *Privateers in Charleston*, v.
[17] Jackson, *Privateers in Charleston*, v.
[18] Jackson, *Privateers in Charleston*, vi.
[19] Jackson, *Privateers in Charleston*, vi.
[20] Jackson, *Privateers in Charleston*, v-vi, 1-11, 48.
[21] Jean-Francois Theric in Melvin H. Jackson, *Privateers in Charleston: 1793-1796* (Washington: Smithsonian Institution Press, 1969), 117.
[22] Theric in Jackson, *Privateers in Charleston*, 117.
[23] Theric in Jackson, *Privateers in Charleston*, 118.
[24] Theric in Jackson, *Privateers in Charleston*, 120.
[25] Theric in Jackson, *Privateers in Charleston*, 121.
[26] Charles Gayarre, *History of Louisiana: The Spanish Domination,* Vol.3 (New Orleans, LA: Armand Hawkins, 1885), 373.
[27] Gayarre, *History of Louisiana*, 373.
[28] "Charleston, Nov. 10," *Aurora General Advertiser*, 30 November 1795.
[29] "Charleston, Nov. 10," *Aurora General Advertiser*, 30 November 1795.
[30] Jackson, *Privateers in Charleston*, 104.
[31] Jackson, *Privateers in Charleston*, 83.
[32] "By Yesterday's Mail," *Impartial Herald*, 18 April 1797.
[33] "By Yesterday's Mail," *Impartial Herald*, 18 April 1797.
[34] "Charleston, Monday, March 20, 1797," *City Gazette*, 20 March 1797.
[35] "By Yesterday's Mail," *Impartial Herald*, 18 April 1797.
[36] "By Yesterday's Mail," *Impartial Herald*, 18 April 1797.
[37] "Charleston, Monday, March 20, 1797," *City Gazette*, 20 March 1797.
[38] "By Yesterday's Mail," *Impartial Herald*, 18 April 1797.
[39] "By Yesterday's Mail," *Impartial Herald*, 18 April 1797.

[40] "By Yesterday's Mail," *Impartial Herald*, 18 April 1797.
[41] *Records of the American Catholic Historical Society of Philadelphia*, Vol 17 (Philadelphia American Catholic Historical Society, 1906), 474.
[42] "List of Letters," *Poulson's American Daily Advertiser*, 03 October 1801.
[43] "Married," *City Gazette*, 23 December 1820.
[44] "Notice," *City Gazette*, 01 December 1821.
[45] Doyle, *The French Revolution*, 47.
[46] Doyle, *The French Revolution*, 56.
[47] Fraser, Jr. *Charleston! Charleston!*, 11.
[48] "Married," *City Gazette*, 23 December 1820.
[49] *Charleston Courier*, 4 October 1856; and Fraser, Jr. *Charleston! Charleston!:* 204.
[50] Paul A. Barra, "Bolchoz name equals Catholicism in Charleston," *The Catholic Miscellany*, 01 January 1998, https://themiscellany.org/1998/01/01/bolchoz-name-equals-catholicism-in-charleston/.
[51] "List of Letters," *City Gazette*, 18 January 1803.
[52] "Bolchoz, Alexander," City Directories for Charleston, South Carolina For the years 1803, 1806, 1807, and 1813, *Ancestry.com*, 25.
[53] "Bolchez, Alexander," City Directories for Charleston, South Carolina For the years 1803, 1806, 1807, and 1813, *Ancestry.com*, 94.
[54] "Marine Register," *Baltimore Price Current*, 30 April 1808; and "Ship News," *Carolina Gazette*, 1 July 1808; and "Ship News," *Charleston Courier*, 21 June 1808.
[55] 1810 U.S. Census.
[56] "South Carolina, Death Records, 1821-1965 for A Bolcos," *Ancestry.com.*
[57] "Charleston Pirate Tour," https://charlestonpiratetour.com/, Accessed 04 February 2020. And Staff Editor, "Pirates of Charleston," *Charleston Harbor Tours*, 24 March 2016, Accessed 04 February 2020, https://www.charlestonharbortours.com/main/charleston-tours-attractions-details/pirates-of-charleston.
[58] "John Cassidy," South Carolina, Death Records, 1821-1965, *Ancestry.com.*

[59] "John Cassidy," Ireland, Catholic Parish Records, 1655-1915, *Ancestry.com.*

[60] "John Cassidy," Ireland, Catholic Parish Records, 1655-1915, *Ancestry.com.*

[61] "John Cassidy," South Carolina, Death Records, 1821-1965, *Ancestry.com.*

[62] Donald M. Williams, *Shamrocks and Pluff Mud: A Glimpse of the Irish in the Southern City of Charleston, South Carolina* (Charleston, SC: Book Surge Publishing, 2005), 11.

[63] Williams, *Shamrocks and Pluff Mud,* 12.

[64] Williams, *Shamrocks and Pluff Mud,* 12-16.

[65] Williams, *Shamrocks and Pluff Mud,* 23-24.

[66] 1860 U.S. Census for John Cassidy, *Ancestry.com.*

[67] "Thomas Monday," Manchester, England, Church of England Marriages and Banns, 1754-1930, *Ancestry.com.*

[68] "Thomas Monday," Manchester, England, Church of England Marriages and Banns, 1754-1930, *Ancestry.com.*

[69] "Thomas Munday," U.K. and U.S. Directories, 1680-1830, *Ancestry.com.*

[70] "Mary Munday," U.S. City Directories, 1822-1995, *Ancestry.com.*

[71] Fraser, Jr. *Charleston! Charleston!,* 244-51.

[72] 1880 U.S. Federal Census for Alexander Duncan, *Ancestry.com.*

[73] "Alexander Duncan," Alabama, Civil War Soldiers, 1860-1865, *Ancestry.com.*

[74] W. Chris Phelps, *Charlestonians in War: The Charleston Battalion* (Gretna: Pelican Publishing Company, 2004), 49.

[75] Phelps, *Charlestonians in War,* 52.

[76] "Dinnis Cassidy," U.S., Confederate Soldiers Compiled Service Records, 1861-1865, *Ancestry.com.*

[77] Phelps, *Charlestonians in War,* 79-98.

[78] "Alexander Duncan," Alabama, Civil War Soldiers, 1860-1865, *Ancestry.com.*

[79] Phelps, *Charlestonians in War,* 103.

[80] "John Cassidy," U.S. Civil War Soldiers, 1861-1865, *Ancestry.com.*

[81] "To the Delegates from the Parishes of St. Philip and St. Michael, in the Convention of the People of the State of South Carolina," *Charleston Mercury,* 29 April 1862.

[82] "John Cassidy," and "C. Cassidy," On the Eve of the Civil War: the Charleston, SC Directories for the Years 1859 and 1860, *Ancestry.com*, 98.
[83] "J Cassidy," U.S. City Directory, 1822-1995, *Ancestry.com* and 1870 U.S. Census for John Cassidy, *Ancestry.com*.
[84] Edward P. Cantwell, *A history of the Charleston police force: From the incorporation of the city, 1783 to 1908* (Charleston: J.J. Furlong, 1908), 2.
[85] Cantwell, *A history of the Charleston police force*, 13.
[86] "Regular Meeting of City Council," *The Charleston Daily News*, 30 November 1870.
[87] "Regular Meeting of City Council," *The Charleston Daily News*, 30 November 1870.
[88] "City Affairs," *The Charleston Daily News*, 13 Dec. 1870.
[89] "John Cassidy," U.S. City Directories, 1822-1995, *Ancestry.com*.
[90] Shepherd W. McKinley, *Stinking Stones and Rocks of Gold: Phosphate, Fertilizer, and Industrialization in Postbellum South Carolina* (Gainesville: University Press of Florida, 2014), 1.
[91] McKinley, *Stinking Stones and Rocks of Gold*, 1.
[92] 1910 U.S. Federal Census for Dennis Cassidy, *Ancestry.com*.
[93] "Charleston- Revolutionary City and Cradle of Secession," *National Park Service*, 15 January 2020, https://www.nps.gov/fosu/index.htm.
[94] "Albin Eissbruckner (#96230), FBI Case Files, Old German Files, 1909-21, *Fold3.com*.
[95] "Albin Eissbruckner (#96230), FBI Case Files, Old German Files, 1909-21, *Fold3.com*.
[96] "Alvin Eisbruckner," U.S. City Directories, 1822-1995, *Ancestry.com* and "Albin Eissbrueckner," U.S. City Directories, 1822-1995, *Ancestry.com*.
[97] 1910 U.S. Federal Census for Albin Eissbruckner, *Ancestry.com*.
[98] In person interview with Carole V. Taylor, given by the author, 06 March 2020.
[99] Katherine L. Turner, *How the Other Half Ate: A History of Working Class Meals at the Turn of the Century* (Berkeley: University of California Press, 2014), 4.

[100] Turner, *How the Other Half Ate*, 61-62.
[101] "J.H. Petermann," New York, Passenger and Crew Lists (including Castle Garden and Ellis Island), 1820-1957, *Ancestry.com*.
[102] "John H. Peterman & Son," U.S. City Directories, 1822-1995, *Ancestry.com*.
[103] "Jacob A. Bertocci," U.S. City Directories, 1822-1995, *Ancestry.com*.
[104] In person interview with Carole V. Taylor, given by the author, 06 March 2020.
[105] Turner, *How the Other Half Ate*, 70-72.
[106] "Eissbruckner," baptismal record, 11 January 1898, Roman Catholic Diocese of Charleston Archives.
[107] "Grand Masquerade Ball," *Charleston News and Courier*, 16 February 1885.
[108] "Maple Grove Dance," *Charleston News and Courier,* 11 May 1906.
[109] "A Grand Masquerade Ball," *Evening Post*, 28 Nov. 1908.
[110] "Preparing for Singing Fest," *The News and Courier*, 2 April 1913.
[111] 1910 U.S. Federal Census for Frederick Heitmann, *Ancestry.com*.
[112] "Society," *Evening Post*, 19 May 1909.
[113] "Dorathea Eissbruckner," South Carolina, Death Records, 1821-1965, *Ancestry.com* and "Funeral Notice," *Charleston News and Courier*, 3 December 1896; and "Funeral Notice," *Charleston News and Courier*, 8 June 1897.
[114] "Eissbruckner," South Carolina, Delayed Birth Records, 1766-1900 and City of Charleston, South Carolina, Birth Records, 1877-1901, 24 November 1897, *Ancestry.com*.
[115] "Mrs. Mattie Eissbruckner," South Carolina, Death Records, 1821-1965, *Ancestry.com*.
[116] "Albin Eissbrückner and Herman Eissbrückner," Charleston Orphan House Index, 1796-1929, Charleston County Public Library.
[117] 1920 U.S. Federal Census for Albern Esbruckner, *Ancestry.com*.
[118] Google maps, "185 East Bay Street," 10 March 2020, https://www.google.com/maps/place/185+E+Bay+St,+Charleston,+SC+29401/@32.7792827,-

79.9270558,3a,75y,281.97h,90t/data=!3m6!1e1!3m4!1siKq6d DbewxZDu-KaMEkDng!2e0!7i16384!8i8192!4m5!3m4!1s0x88fe7a0e820 099af:0xce01aef50ab4941b!8m2!3d32.7793283!4d-79.9274247.

[119] T.J. Parsell, "Forward," in *Uptown Down South Cuisine: Magnolias Restaurant* (Layton: Gibbs Smith, 2015), written by Don Drake.

[120] Parsell, "Forward."

[121] "About," *Charleston Wine and Food*, Accessed 10 March 2020, https://charlestonwineandfood.com/about/.

Endnotes for Chapter 2

[1] Beyer, Catherine. 2019. *The Jedi Code's Four Truths.* 27 March 2020. https://www.learnreligions.com/the-jedi-code-95910.

[2] Ancestry.com. 2013. *Harris Family History.* https://www.ancestry.com/name-origin?surname=harris.; Barb. 2010. *Harris Family History.* 9 March 2020. http://historyharrisfamily.blogspot.com/2010/03/harris-family-crest.html.; Forebears. 2012. *Harris Surname Origin, Meaning & Last Name History.* https://forebears.io/surnames/harris#meaning.; House of Names. 2014-2018. *Harris History, Family Crest & Coats of Arms.* https://www.houseofnames.com/harris-family-crest.; Powell, Kimberly. 2019. *Harris Surname Meaning and Origin.* 8 March 2020. https://www.thoughtco.com/harris-name-meaning-and-origin-1422523.; SurnameDB. 2017. *Last name: Harris.* https://www.surnamedb.com/Surname/Harris.

[3] Ancestry.com. 2013. *Harris Family History.*; Barb. 2010. *Harris Family History.* 9 March 2020; Ancestry.com. 2012. *Harris Surname Origin, Meaning & Last Name History.*

[4] Ancestry.com. 2013. *Harris Family History.*; Ancestry.com. 2014-2018. *Harris History, Family Crest & Coats of Arms.*; Powell, Kimberly. 2019. *Harris Surname Meaning and Origin.* 8 March 2020.

[5] Ancestry.com. 2013. *Harris Family History.*; Barb. 2010. *Harris Family History.* 9 March 2020.

[6] See Bernard Burke, *The General Armory of England, Scotland, Ireland and Wales; Comprising A Registry of*

Armorial Bearings from the Earliest to the Present Time (London: Harrison & Sons, 1884).

[7] "Merriam-Webster.com Dictionary." *s.v. "heraldry".* https://www.merriam-webster.com/dictionary/heraldry.

[8] Arturo R. Lobato, "A General Survey of Heraldry," *Artes De México,* 126, (1970), 34.

[9] Lobato, "A General Survey of Heraldry," 34.

[10] George Bellew, "Modern Heraldry," *Journal of the Royal Society of Arts,* 111 (1963), 80; and J. Shelton Mackenzie, "Heraldry and Genealogy," *Cosmopolitan Art Journal,* 4:2, (1860), 60-62.

[11] Bellew, "Modern Heraldry," 80.; Mackenzie, "Heraldry and Genealogy," 60-62.

[12] Lobato, "A General Survey of Heraldry," 43; Ailfrid Mac Lochlainn, "The Interpretation of Heraldry," *Journal of the County Louth Archaeological Society,* 12:4 (1952), 242.

[13] Stratton O. Hammon, "Knighthood Is Still in Flower," *The Register of the Kentucky Historical Society,* 64:3 (1966). 243.

[14] Hammon, "Knighthood Is Still in Flower," 243.

[15] Burke, *The General Armory of England, Scotland, Ireland and Wales,* xxviii.

[16] Burke, *The General Armory of England, Scotland, Ireland and Wales,* xxxii-xxxiii; Lochlainn, "The Interpretation of Heraldry," 239.

[17] Burke, *The General Armory of England, Scotland, Ireland and Wales,* 458-460.

[18] S. T. Aveling, *Heraldry: Ancient and Modern: Including Boutell's Heraldry Edited and Revised, With Additions* (London: Frederick Warne and Co., 1873), 11-13, 89. https://archive.org/details/heraldryancientm00bout/page/n5/mode/2up.; Burke, *The General Armory of England, Scotland, Ireland and Wales,* xxix; W. Cecil Wade, *The Symbolisms of Heraldry* (London: George Redway, 1898), 35-37, 69.

[19] Aveling, *Heraldry: Ancient and Modern. Including Boutell's Heraldry Edited and Revised,* 11-13; Burke, *The General Armory of England, Scotland, Ireland and Wales,* xxviii-xxix, xxxv; Wade, *The Symbolisms of Heraldry,* 35-37.

[20] Aveling, S. T. 1873. *Heraldry: Ancient and Modern,* 89; Burke, *The General Armory of England, Scotland, Ireland and Wales,* 458-460; Wade, *The Symbolisms of Heraldry,* 69.

[21]Aveling, *Heraldry: Ancient and Modern. Including Boutell's Heraldry Edited and Revised,* 89; Burke, *The General Armory of England, Scotland, Ireland and Wales,* xxxviii; and Wade, *The Symbolisms of Heraldry,* 69.

[22] Aveling, *Heraldry: Ancient and Modern. Including Boutell's Heraldry Edited and Revised,* 133; Burke, *The General Armory of England, Scotland, Ireland and Wales,* xxxvii, 458-460; Lobato, "A General Survey of Heraldry," 46.; Wade, *The Symbolisms of Heraldry,* 106-107.

[23] James Harmon, *Re: NC, Lucy, Robert, John Harris, late 1700s.* 6 April 2004, https://www.genealogy.com/forum/surnames/topics/harris/17752/ ; Our Family Roots. 2012. "Our Family Roots (Thompson Harris III)." *Compilation of Strickland, Westberry, Bennett, and Strickland Families.* Compiled by Our Family Roots. http://ourfamroots.info/westberry-family/rev-moses-sr/julia-ann-westberry/thompson-harris/.

[24] Ancestry.com. 2020. "Harris Family Tree." *Harris Family Tree: The Harris, Capps, Barnes, and Early Families.* Compiled by Jesse Quentin Harris. Charleston, South Carolina: Ancestry.com Operations, Inc., March 1. https://www.ancestry.com/family-tree/tree/166975071/family/familyview?cfpid=272167244739&selnode=1.; —. 2012. "Our Family Roots."

[25] Ancestry.com. 2012. "Our Family Roots."

[26] Ancestry.com. 2020. "Harris Family Tree."

[27] Ancestry.com. 2020. "Harris Family Tree."

[28] United States Census Bureau. *1850 Overview - History - U.S. Census Bureau.* 17 December 2020. https://www.census.gov/history/www/through_the_decades/overview/1850.html.

[29] Google Maps. 2020. *Directions to/Distance Between Burke, Laurens, Appling, Lowndes, Lanier, and Clinch Counties, Georgia.* April 6. https://www.google.com/maps; Ancestry.com. 2012. "Our Family Roots."

[30] Ancestry.com. 2020. "Harris Family Tree."

[31] Ancestry.com. 2012. "Our Family Roots."

[32] Ancestry.com. 2020. "Harris Family Tree."

[33] Ware County Board of Commissioners, *Ware County, Georgia,* 2020, http://www.warecounty.com/About-Us.aspx.

[34] U.S. Census Bureau. 1850-1853. *1850 Census: The Seventh Census of the United States.* https://www.census.gov/library/publications/1853/dec/1850a.html; Ancestry.com. *1850 Overview - History - U.S. Census Bureau,* 17 December 2019.

[35] Ancestry.com. 2012. "Our Family Roots."

[36] U.S. Census Bureau. 1850-1853. *1850 Census: The Seventh Census of the United States.*

[37] Ancestry.com. 2020. "Harris Family Tree."

[38] Ancestry.com. 2012. "Our Family Roots."

[39] Ancestry.com. 2020. "Harris Family Tree."

[40] Google Maps, *Directions to/Distance Between Burke, Laurens, Appling, Lowndes, Lanier, and Clinch Counties, Georgia.* 6 April 2020.

[41] Ancestry.com. 2020. "Harris Family Tree."; Ancestry.com. 2012. "Our Family Roots."

[42] Colonial Williamsburg. 2020. *Wheelwright: Trades.* https://www.colonialwilliamsburg.org/locations/wheelwright/.

[43] "A Wheelwright of Charlestown," *Bulletin of the Business Historical Society,* 5:6, (1931), 6-9. doi:10.2307/3110606.; Colonial Williamsburg. 2020. *Wheelwright: Trades.*

[44] Ancestry.com. 2012. "Our Family Roots."

[45]Ancestry.com. 2020. "Harris Family Tree."

[46] Ancestry.com. 2020. "Harris Family Tree."; Ancestry.com. 2012. "Our Family Roots (George W. Harris)." *Compilation of Strickland, Westberry, Bennett, and Strickland Families.* Compiled by Our Family Roots. http://ourfamroots.info/westberry-family/rev-moses-sr/julia-ann-westberry/.

[47] Ancestry.com. 2012. "Our Family Roots."

[48] Ancestry.com. 2020. "Harris Family Tree."; Ancestry.com. 2012. "Our Family Roots (George W. Harris)."; Ray City Community Library, *Ray City History Blog.* 8 May 2013, https://raycityhistory.wordpress.com/tag/james-harris/.

[49] Ancestry.com. 2012. "Our Family Roots (George W. Harris)."; Ray City Community Library. 2013. *Ray City History Blog.* May 8.

[50] Ancestry.com. 2020. "Harris Family Tree."; Ancestry.com. 2012. "Our Family Roots."; Ray City Community Library. 2013. *Ray City History Blog.* 8 May 2020.

[51] Ancestry.com. 2020. "Harris Family Tree."; Ancestry.com. 2012. "Our Family Roots (James Harris)." *Compilation of Strickland, Westberry, Bennett, and Strickland Families.* Compiled by Our Family Roots. http://ourfamroots.info/westberry-family/rev-moses-sr/julia-ann-westberry/james-harris/; and Ray City Community Library. 2013. *Ray City History Blog.*

[52] Ancestry.com. 2020. "Harris Family Tree."; Ancestry.com. 2012. "Our Family Roots (James Harris)"; Ray City Community Library. *Ray City History Blog.* 8 May 2020.

[53] Ray City Com. Library. 2013. *Ray City History Blog.* 8 May

[54] Harris, Jesse Quentin, ed. 2020. "Harris and Capps Family Archives." *Harris and Capps Family Archives, Private Collection.* Compiled by Arthur Phillip Harris, Susie Louise Conner Harris Johnson, Laura Anna Capps Harris and Jesse Quentin Harris. Charleston, South Carolina.

[55] Jesse Quentin Harris, ed. "Harris and Capps Family Archives" 2020; Google Maps. 2020.

[56] Harris, "Harris and Capps Family Archives."

[57] Harris, "Harris and Capps Family Archives."; Ancestry.com. 2012. "Our Family Roots (James Harris)."; Ray City Community Library. 2013. *Ray City History Blog.*

[58] Harris, "Harris and Capps Family Archives."

[59] Harris, "Harris and Capps Family Archives."; Ancestry.com. 2012. "Our Family Roots (James Harris)."

[60] Ancestry.com. 2020. "Harris Family Tree."; Harris, Jesse Quentin, ed. 2020. "Harris and Capps Family Archives."; Ancestry.com. 2012. "Our Family Roots (James Harris)."

[61] Harris, "Harris and Capps Family Archives."

[62] Legacy.com. 2008. *Susie Conner Harris Johnson.* January 20. https://www.legacy.com/obituaries/name/susie-johnson-obituary?pid=101671364.

[63] Harris, "Harris and Capps Family Archives."

[64] *Barnes and Early Family Archives, Private Collection*; Harris, "Harris and Capps Family Archives."

[65] Ancestry.com. 2013. *Capps Family History.* https://www.ancestry.com/name-origin?surname=capps.; —. 2014-2018. *Capps Name Meaning, Family History, Family Crest & Coats of Arms.* https://www.houseofnames.com/capps-family-crest.; Origin of

Names. 2019. *Capps Family Crest/Capps Coat of Arms.* 23 November 2020, http://www.4crests.com/capps-coat-of-arms.html; Ancestry.com. 2017. *Last Name: Capps.* https://www.surnamedb.com/Surname/Capps.

[66] Aveling, *Heraldry: Ancient and Modern. Including Boutell's Heraldry Edited and Revised,* 11-16.; Burke, *The General Armory of England, Scotland, Ireland and Wales,* xxviii-xxix.; Wade, *The Symbolisms of Heraldry,* 35-37.

[67] Ancestry.com. 2020. "Harris Family Tree."

[68] John D. Light, "A Dictionary of Blacksmithing Terms," *Historical Archaeology,* 41:2, (2007), 84-157.

[69] Ancestry.com. 2020. "Harris Family Tree."

[70] W.C. Shiel, *Medical Definition of Dropsy,* 26 January 2017, www.medicinenet.com/script/main/art.asp?articlekey=13311.

[71] Ancestry.com. 2020. "Harris Family Tree."

[72] Ancestry.com. 2020. "Harris Family Tree."

[73] Ancestry.com. 2020. "Harris Family Tree."; Jesse Greenspan, 2020; Ancestry.com. 1850-1853. *1850 Census: The Seventh Census of the United States*; Ancestry.com. 2019. *1850 Overview - History - U.S. Census Bureau.* 17 Dec. 2020.

[74] Ancestry.com. 2020. "Harris Family Tree."

[75] *Barnes and Early Family Archives, Private Collection*; Harris, "Harris and Capps Family Archives."

[76] Ancestry.com. 2013. *Early Family History.* https://www.ancestry.com/name-origin?surname=early.; —. 2012. *Early Surname Origin, Meaning & Last Name History.* https://forebears.io/surnames/early#meaning.; Ancestry.com. 2014-2018. *Early Name Meaning, Family History, Family Crest & Coats of Arms.* https://www.houseofnames.com/early-family-crest.; Irish Nation. 2019. *Early Coat of Arms, Family Crest.* http://www.irishsurnames.com/cgi-bin/gallery.pl?name=early&capname=Early&letter=e.; Ancestry.com. 2017. *Last Name: Early.* https://www.surnamedb.com/Surname/Early.

[77] Burke, *The General Armory of England, Scotland, Ireland and Wales,* 312.

[78] Aveling, *Heraldry: Ancient and Modern. Including Boutell's Heraldry Edited and Revised,* 94-95.; Lobato, "A General Survey of Heraldry," 49; and Wade, *The Symbolisms of Heraldry,* 83-84.

[79] Ancestry.com. 2020. "Harris Family Tree."
[80] Ancestry.com. 2020. "Harris Family Tree."; *Barnes and Early Family Archives, Private Collection.*; Harris, Jesse Quentin, ed. 2020. "Harris and Capps Family Archives."
[81] Ancestry.com. 2020. "Harris Family Tree."; *Barnes and Early Family Archives, Private Collection.*; Harris, Jesse Quentin, ed. 2020. "Harris and Capps Family Archives."
[82] Parker, et. al., 2020. "Harris Family Tree."
[83] Ancestry.com. 2020. "Harris Family Tree."; *Barnes and Early Family Archives, Private Collection.*; Harris, Jesse Quentin, ed. 2020. "Harris and Capps Family Archives."
[84] Ancestry.com. 2020. "Harris Family Tree."; *Barnes and Early Family Archives, Private Collection.*; Harris, Jesse Quentin, ed. 2020. "Harris and Capps Family Archives."
[85] Ancestry.com. 2020. "Harris Family Tree."
[86] *Barnes and Early Family Archives, Private Collection;* Bond, "Retirement Ahead"; and Parker, et. al., *The Ahoskie Era of Hertford County.*
[87] *Barnes and Early Family Archives, Private Collection.;* and Bond, "Retirement Ahead."
[88] Bond, "Retirement Ahead."
[89] *Barnes and Early Family Archives, Private Collection.*
[90] *Barnes and Early Family Archives, Private Collection.*
[91] *Barnes and Early Family Archives, Private Collection.;* Harris, ed. "Harris and Capps Family Archives."
[92] All Family Crests. 2015. *Barnes Family Crest and Meaning of the Coat of Arms for the Surname.* http://www.allfamilycrests.com/b/barnes-family-crest-coat-of-arms.shtml.; Ancestry.com. 2013. *Barnes Family History.* https://www.ancestry.com/name-origin?surname=barnes; Ancestry.com. 2012. *Barnes Surname Origin, Meaning & Last Name History.* https://forebears.io/surnames/barnes#meaning; Ancestry.com. 2014-2018. *Barnes History, Family Crest & Coats of Arms.* https://www.houseofnames.com/barnes-family-crest; Joy Empire Inc. 2015. *Barnes Family Crest, Coat of Arms and Name History.* https://coadb.com/surnames/barnes-arms.html.; Ancestry.com. 2017. *Last Name: Barnes.* https://www.surnamedb.com/Surname/Barnes

[93] Burke, *The General Armory of England, Scotland, Ireland and Wales,* 49-50.

[94] Aveling, *Heraldry: Ancient and Modern. Including Boutell's Heraldry Edited and Revised,* 167; Lobato, "A General Survey of Heraldry," 49; and Wade, *The Symbolisms of Heraldry,* 65.

[95] Ancestry.com. 2020. "Harris Family Tree."; *Behind the Name - the etymology and history of first names: Sarah.* December 14. http://www.behindthename.com/name/sarah.

[96] Ancestry.com. 2020. "Harris Family Tree."

[97] Ancestry.com. 2020. "Harris Family Tree."

[98] Ancestry.com. 2020. "Harris Family Tree."; *Barnes and Early Family Archives, Private Collection.*

[99] Ancestry.com. 2020. "Harris Family Tree."; *Barnes and Early Family Archives, Private Collection.*

[100] *Barnes and Early Family Archives, Private Collection.*

[101] Ancestry.com. 2020. "Harris Family Tree."; *Barnes and Early Family Archives, Private Collection.; The Herald,* "Barnes-Sawyer Ahoskie's First Big Wholesale Distributing Unit." 1 January 1959, 7, http://newspapers.digitalnc.org/lccn/sn84020678/1959-01-01/ed-1/seq-7/#.

[102] Ancestry.com. 2020. "Harris Family Tree."; *Barnes and Early Family Archives, Private Collection.*

[103] *Barnes and Early Family Archives, Private Collection.; The Herald.* n.d. "World War II Interrupted But J. W. Barnes Nears CPA Dreams."

[104] *Barnes and Early Family Archives, Private Collection.; The Herald.* n.d. "World War II Interrupted But J. W. Barnes Nears CPA Dreams."

[105] Staff Writer, *Consolidated B-24 Liberator: Four-Engined Strategic Heavy Bomber Aircraft,* 30 July 2019, www.militaryfactory.com/aircraft/detail.asp?aircraft_id=80.

[106] *Barnes and Early Family Archives, Private Collection;* and "World War II Interrupted But J. W. Barnes Nears CPA Dreams," *The Herald.* n.d.

[107] *Barnes and Early Family Archives, Private Collection;* and "World War II Interrupted But J. W. Barnes Nears CPA Dreams," *The Herald.* n.d.

[108] *Barnes and Early Family Archives, Private Collection.*

[109] Joseph Amato, "Rethinking Family History." *Minnesota History*, 60:8, (2007/2008), 326-33.

[110] Samuel M. Otterstrom and Brian E. Bunker, "Genealogy, Migration, and the Intertwined Geographies of Personal Pasts" in *Annals of the Association of American Geographers*, 103:3, (2013), 549-50.

[111] Matthew Elliott, "The Inconvenient Ancestor: Slavery and Selective Remembrance on Genealogy Television," *Studies in Popular Culture*, 39:2, (2017), 73-90.

[112] Sheehan-Dean, "The Long Civil War 113.

[113] Aaron Sheehan-Dean, "The Long Civil War: A Historiography of the Consequences of the Civil War," *The Virginia Magazine of History and Biography*, 119:2, (2011), 106-53.

[114] Rayna Rapp, Ellen Ross, and Renate Bridenthal, "Examining Family History," *Feminist Studies*, 5:1, (1979), 181-83, doi:10.2307/3177554.

[115] Rapp, Ross, and Bridenthal, "Examining Family History," 181-83,

[116] James C. Boyles, "Under a Spreading Chestnut-Tree": The Blacksmith and His Forge in Nineteenth-Century American Art," *The Journal of the Society for Industrial Archeology*, 34:1/2, (2008), 9-24.

[117] John Williams-Davies, "The Changing Role of the Rural Blacksmith," *Oral History*, 18:2, (1990), 68-69.

[118] Barbara S. Griffith, "A Case Study in Textiles: Defeat at Kannapolis," In *The Crisis of American Labor: Operation Dixie and the Defeat of the CIO*, (1988), 46-50, doi:10.2307/j.ctv941x0c.8.; Cynthia D. Anderson, Michael D. Schulman, and Phillip J. Wood, "Globalization and Uncertainty: The Restructuring of Southern Textiles," *Social Problems*, 48:4, (2001), 484. doi:10.1525/sp.2001.48.4.478.

[119] "Lexico Powered by Oxford." *s.v. "paternalism",* 2020. https://www.lexico.com/en/definition/paternalism.

[120] Leon Fink, "When Community Comes Homes to Roost: The Southern Milltown as Lost Cause," *Journal of Social History,* 40:1, (2006), 136.

[121] Griffith, "A Case Study in Textiles, 46-50.

Endnotes for Chapter 3

[1] William Rutledge, *An Illustrated History of Yadkin County, 1850-1965* (Yadkinville, NC: self-published, 1965), 69.

[2] Dale Sanderson, "End of US Highway 21," 4 July 4, 2009, unpublished.

[3] See C. H. Liebs, *Main Street to Miracle Mile* (Baltimore, Johns Hopkins Press, 1995).

[4] Liebs, *Main Street to Miracle Mile.*

[5] See T. Vale and G. Vale, *U.S. 40 Today: Thirty years of landscape change in America* (Madison, University of Wisconsin Press, 1983).

[6] Liebs, *Main Street to Miracle Mile*

[7] Mark Royall, Interview, Bradenton, Florida, 15 March 2020.

[8] Hubert "Papaw" Royall. Interview, 15 March 2020.

[9] Jeffrey Royall, "Back Woods Hunt Club," *Back Woods Hunt Club*. 17 April 2020. *http://www.backwoodshuntclub.com/*.

[10] U.S. Department of the Interior, U.S. Fish and Wildlife Service, and U.S. Department of Commerce, U.S. Census Bureau. 2016 National Survey of Fishing, Hunting, and Wildlife-Associated Recreation.

[11] The State Conservation Machine, *Association of Fish & Wildlife Agencies, Arizona Game and Fish Department.* 2017.

[12] Fish & Wildlife, Sustaining and Connecting People to A Looming Crisis Can be Avoided. *A Recommendation of the Blue Ribbon Panel on Sustaining America's Diverse Fish and Wildlife Resources*. Blue Ribbon Panel. Michigan Department of Natural Resources Wildlife Division.

[13] Kimberly L. Dawe and Stan Boutin, "Climate Change Is the Primary Driver of White-Tailed Deer (*Odocoileus Virginianus*) Range Expansion at the Northern Extent of Its Range; Land Use Is Secondary," US National Library of Medicine National Institutes of Health (Hoboken, NJ: John Wiley and Sons Inc., 2016).

[14] Duane Diefenbach, "Will Climate Change Change Deer? (Deer-Forest Study)," Deer-Forest Study (Penn State University). 2020 Penn State University. Department of Ecosystem Science and Management, 7 May 2015.

[15] Diefenbach, "Will Climate Change Change Deer? (Deer-Forest Study)."

[16] Marion N. Nugent, *Cavaliers and Pioneers: Abstracts of Virginia Land Patents and Grants, 1623-1666,* Vol. 1 (Richmond, VA: Dietz Printing Co., 1934), 767.
[17] Hubert "Papaw" Royall. Interview, 15 March 2020.
[18] Hubert "Papaw" Royall. Interview, 15 March 2020.
[19] Hubert "Papaw" Royall. Interview, 15 March 2020.
[20] 300 Acres. Henrico Co. p. 452
[21] Source number: 317.000; Source type: Electronic Database; Number of Pages: 1; Submitter Code: LCW
[22] Katherine Isham-Banks, "Will of Katherine Isham-Banks," 1686. Retrieved from family collection.
[23] "Virginia Landmarks Register," Virginia Department of Historic Resources. 21 September 2013.
[24] Historical Marker, "Richmond: The James River Plantations". Virginia Department of Historic Places.
[25] Ancestry.com. *U.S., Find A Grave Index, 1600s-Current* [database on-line]. Provo, UT, USA: Ancestry.com Operations, Inc., 2012.
[26] Ancestry.com. *U.S., Find A Grave Index, 1600s-Current* [database on-line]. Provo, UT, USA: Ancestry.com Operations, Inc., 2012.
[27] A. Coates, ed., *Talks to Students and Teachers* (Chapel Hill: Creative Printers, 1971).
[28] Scott Dickson, *In Search of Mayberry* (Boone, NC: Parkway Publishers, Inc., 2005), 75.
[29] "Stone Mountain State Park," *Stone Mountain State Park | NC State Parks*. North Carolina Division of Parks and Recreation, n.d.
[30] Object Label, *Hutchinson Homestead,* Stone Mountain State Park, North Carolina.
[31] Object Label, *Hutchinson Homestead.*
[32] J.D. Lewis, *Surry County, NC* (Self-Published, 2020).
[33] Will of Henry Royall. Retrieved from Family Collection. 1828, Surry County, North Carolina.
[34] Ancestry.com. *U.S., Find A Grave Index, 1600s-Current* [database on-line]. Provo, UT, USA: Ancestry.com Operations, Inc., 2012.
[35] 1850 Census Place: South Division, Surry, North Carolina; Roll: 646; Page: 217A

[36] 1860 Census Place: Yadkin, North Carolina; Page: 325; Family History Library Film: 803919
[37] "Census of Population and Housing". Census.gov.
[38] Frances H. Casstevens, *The Civil War and Yadkin County, North Carolina: A History* (Jefferson, NC: McFarland and Co., Inc., 2006), 15.
[39] Casstevens, *The Civil War and Yadkin County,* 15.
[40] Casstevens, *The Civil War and Yadkin County,* 55.
[41] Casstevens, *The Civil War and Yadkin County,* 13.
[42] Casstevens, *The Civil War and Yadkin County,* 14.
[43] Casstevens, *The Civil War and Yadkin County,* 15.
[44] John C. Inscoe and Gordon B. McKinney, *The Heart of Confederate Appalachia: Western North Carolina in the Civil War* (Chapel Hill: University of North Carolina Press, 2003), 9.
[45] 1860 Census Place: Yadkin, North Carolina; Page: 325; Family History Library Film: 803919
[46] Casstevens, *The Civil War and Yadkin County,* 62.
[47] Casstevens, *The Civil War and Yadkin County,* 63.
[48] Rutledge, *An Illustrated History of Yadkin County.*
[49] Casstevens, *The Civil War and Yadkin County,* 259.
[50] Charles C. Bolton, *Poor Whites of the Antebellum South: Tenants and Laborers in Central North Carolina and Northeast Mississippi* (Durham, NC: Duke University Press, 1993), 2.
[51] Shallow Ford Historic Marker. Shallowford Road, Huntsville, NC, 2011. NC Office of Archives and History.
[52] Bolton, *Poor Whites of the Antebellum South,* 4.
[53] Bolton, *Poor Whites of the Antebellum South,* 14.
[54] Gunnar Myrdal, *An American Dilemma: The Negro Problem and Modern Democracy* (New York: Harper & Row, 1969), 1354.
[55] C. Vann Woodward, *The Origins of the New South* (Baton Rouge: Louisiana State University Press, 1951).
[56] Amy Dru Stanley, *From Bondage to Contract: Wage Labor, Marriage, and the Market in the Age of Slave Emancipation* (Chicago: University of Chicago Press, 1998).
[57] Woodward, *The Origins of the New South.*
[58] Henry Grady, *The New South,* (New York: Robert Bonner's Sons, 1890), 19.

[59] Frank Tursi, *Winston-Salem: A History* (Winston-Salem, NC: J.F. Blair, 1994), 110–11.
[60] Tursi, *Winston-Salem,* 196-97.
[61] Barry McGee, "R. J. Reynolds Tobacco Company," in *Encyclopedia of North Carolina* (Chape Hill: University of North Carolina Press, 2006).
[62] W. O. Absher and Nancy W. Simpson, *The Heritage of Wilkes County* (North Wilkesboro, NC: Wilkes Genealogical Society in cooperation with Hunter Publishing Co., 1982), 2.
[63] Aaron E. Lancaster, *Chasing the Good Ol' Boys and Girls of Wilkes County, North Carolina* (MA Thesis, Appalachian State University, 2013).
[64] Lancaster, *Chasing the Good Ol' Boys and Girls of Wilkes County,* 4.
[65] Lancaster, *Chasing the Good Ol' Boys and Girls of Wilkes County,* 5.
[66] Lancaster, *Chasing the Good Ol' Boys and Girls of Wilkes County,* 6, 93.

Endnotes for Chapter 4

[1] Childhood memory by the author.
[2] Avi Astor, Marian Burchardt, and Mar Griera, "The Politics of Religious Heritage: Framing Claims to Religion as Culture in Spain," *Journal for the Scientific Study of Religion,* 56:1, (2017), 126-42. doi:10.1111/jssr.12321.
[3] Tsivolas Theodosios, "The Legal Foundations of Religious Cultural Heritage Protection," *Religions,* 10:4, (2019), 283. doi:10.3390/rel10040283.
[4] Theodosios, "The Legal Foundations of Religious Cultural Heritage Protection," 283.
[5] Theodosios, "The Legal Foundations of Religious Cultural Heritage Protection," 283.
[6] Theodosios, "The Legal Foundations of Religious Cultural Heritage Protection," 283.
[7] Theodosios, "The Legal Foundations of Religious Cultural Heritage Protection," 283.
[8] Silvia De Ascaniis and Lorenzo Cantoni, "Online Visit Opinions about Attractions of the Religious Heritage: An Argumentative Approach," *Church, Communication and Culture,* 2:2, (2017), 179-202.

[9] "National Register Database and Research." National Parks Service. U.S. Department of the Interior, 18 April 2020. https://www.nps.gov/subjects/nationalregister/database-research.htm.

[10] De Ascaniis, and Cantoni, "Online Visit Opinions about Attractions of the Religious Heritage," 179–202.

[11] Mihaela Manila, "Religious Heritage, an Important Element in Creating an Identity of Vrancea County Tourism," *Revista de Turism,* 12 (December 2011), 33-38.

[12] Manila, "Religious Heritage, an Important Element in Creating an Identity of Vrancea County Tourism," 33-38.

[13] De Ascaniis, and Cantoni, "Online Visit Opinions about Attractions of the Religious Heritage," 179-202.

[14] August R. Suelflow. "Preserving Church Historical Resources," *The American Archivist,* 28:2, (1965), 239.

[15] Suelflow, "Preserving Church Historical Resources," 239.

[16] Suelflow, "Preserving Church Historical Resources," 239.

[17] Karen Davison and Jenny Russell, "Disused Religious Space: Youth Participation in Built Heritage Regeneration," *Religions*, 8:6, (2020), 4.

[18] Davison and Russell, "Disused Religious Space," 4.

[19] Davison and Russell, "Disused Religious Space," 4.

[20] Olimpia Niglio, "Knowing, Preserving and Enhancing. The Cultural-Religious Heritage," *Almatourism,* 8:15, (2017), 152-56. doi:10.6092/issn.2036-5195/7158.

[21] Georgios Alexopoulos, "Living Religious Heritage and Challenges to Museum Ethics: Reflections from the Monastic Community of Mount Athos," *Journal of Conservation and Museum Studies,* 11:1, (2013), doi:10.5334/jcms.1021208.

[22] Alexopoulos, "Living Religious Heritage and Challenges to Museum Ethics."

[23] Suelflow, "Preserving Church Historical Resources," 240.

[24] Jewel L. Spangler, "Becoming Baptists: Conversion in Colonial and Early National Virginia," *The Journal of Southern History,* 67:2, (2001), 243-86. doi:10.2307/3069866.

[25] Klotter, *Our Kentucky,* 93.

[26] National Register of Historic Places, Providence Baptist Church, Winchester, Clark County, Kentucky, National Register #76000864.

[27] National Register of Historic Places, Providence Baptist Church, Winchester, Clark County, Kentucky, National Register #76000864.
[28] Andrew Patrick, "Daniel Boone, Surveyor / Bush Settlement," *ExploreKYHistory*, 16 January 2020, https://explorekyhistory.ky.gov/items/show/824
[29] Lowell H. Harrison, *Kentucky's Road to Statehood* (Lexington: The University Press of Kentucky, 2015), 5.
[30] James C. Klotter, *Our Kentucky: A Study of the Bluegrass State*. Vol. 2nd ed. (Lexington: The University Press of Kentucky, 2015), 93.
[31] Family Documents.
[32] Edwin Erle Sparks, *The American Historical Review,* 9:1, (1903), 160-63, doi:10.2307/1834238.
[33] Sparks, *The American Historical Review,* 162.
[34] National Register of Historic Places, Providence Baptist Church, Winchester, Clark County, Kentucky, National Register #76000864.
[35] Pearson, J. Stephen, "Biblical Typology as Oppositional Historiography in Fray Angelico Chavez's From an Altar Screen," *The Journal of the Society for the Study of the Multi-Ethnic Literature of the United States,* 42:3, (2017), 152-75.
[36] Stephen, "Biblical Typology as Oppositional Historiography in Fray Angelico Chavez's From an Altar Screen," 152–75.
[37] Family Book.
[38] Acts 17:30 (KJV)
[39] Ephesians 2:8 (KJV).
[40] 1 Corinthians 15:1-3 (KJV)
[41] Stephen, "Biblical Typology as Oppositional Historiography in Fray Angelico Chavez's From an Altar Screen," 152–75
[42] National Register of Historic Places, Providence Baptist Church, Winchester, Clark County, Kentucky, National Register #76000864.
[43] National Register of Historic Places, Providence Baptist Church, Winchester, Clark County, Kentucky, National Register #76000864.
[44] National Register of Historic Places, Providence Baptist Church, Winchester, Clark County, Kentucky, National Register #76000864.
[45] Family Records.

[46] National Register of Historic Places, Providence Baptist Church, Winchester, Clark County, Kentucky, National Register #76000864.

[47] National Register of Historic Places, Providence Baptist Church, Winchester, Clark County, Kentucky, National Register #76000864.

Endnotes for Chapter 5

[1] Photograph of Cara Quigley at the beach in Galveston, Texas as a child, Quigley Family Papers, 2000.

[2] "Galveston Island Beach Patrol," https://www.galvestonislandbeachpatrol.com/about-us/

[3] "Spanish Explorer Cabeza De Vaca Lands in Texas," HISTORY. A&E Television Networks,
16 November 2009. https://www.history.com/this-day-in-history/cabeza-de-vaca-discovers-texas.

[4] "Spanish Explorer Cabeza De Vaca Lands in Texas," 2009.

[5] "Jean Lafitte's Maison Rouge," *Galveston Ghost*, 28 January 2020, http://www.galvestonghost.com/MaisonRouge.html.

[6] Harris Gaylord, Warren "LAFFITE, JEAN," Historical Association and the University of Texas. 28 January 2020. https://tshaonline.org/handbook/online/articles/fla12.

[7] "Jean Lafitte's Maison Rouge."

[8] "History of the City of Galveston," Mitchell Historic Properties, www.mitchellhistoricproperties.com/a-look-back-on-the-city-of-galveston-tx-and-the-rich-history-it-harbors/

[9] "10 Historical Facts You Probably Don't Know About Galveston," *Galveston.com*, 2015, https://www.galveston.com/blog/659/10-historical-facts-you-probably-dont-know-about-galveston/

[10] Becky Little, "How the Galveston Hurricane of 1900 Became the Deadliest U.S. Natural Disaster," *HISTORY*, 29 August 2017. https://www.history.com/news/how-the-galveston-hurricane-of-1900-became-the-deadliest-u-s-natural-disaster

[11] Little, "How the Galveston Hurricane of 1900 Became the Deadliest U.S. Natural Disaster."

[12] "The Sisters of Charity Orphanage," *The 1900 Storm: Galveston Newspaper Inc.*, 2014. https://www.1900storm.com/orphanage.html.

[13] "Hurricane Damage, Galveston, USA, 1900," Library of Congress/ Science Photo Library. https://www.sciencephoto.com/media/163820/view

[14] Little, How the Galveston Hurricane of 1900 Became the Deadliest U.S. Natural Disaster."

[15] "Galveston Seawall and Grade Raising Project."

[16] John Burnett, "The Tempest At Galveston: 'We Knew There Was A Storm Coming, But We Had No Idea'." *NPR- South Carolina Public Radio*, 30 Nov. 2017, https://www.npr.org/2017/11/30/566950355/the-tempest-at-galveston-we-knew-there-was-a-storm-coming-but-we-had-no-idea.

[17] "Galveston Seawall and Grade Raising Project," *American Society of Civil Engineers*, 3 February 2020, https://www.asce.org/project/galveston-seawall-and-grade-raising-project/.

[18] "Construction of the Galveston Seawall 1902," *Reddit*, https://www.reddit.com/r/texas/comments/b7sstd/construction_of_the_galveston_seawall_1902/

[19] Marilyn Harper and Ron Thomson, "Telling the Stories: Planning the Effective Programs for Properties in the National Register of Historic Places," U.S. Department of the Interior, National Park Service- National Register, History and Education. 2000.

[20] Harper and Thomson, Telling the Stories."

[21] Harper and Thomson, Telling the Stories."

[22] Harper and Thomson, Telling the Stories."

[23] Robert E. Goodin and Charles Tilly, *The Oxford handbook of Contextual Political Analysis* (Oxford University Press, 2006), 213-14.

[24] Goodin and Tilly, *The Oxford handbook of Contextual Political Analysis,* 213-14.

[25] Ben Walsh, "Case Study 4 Background: The End of the British Empire in Ireland." The National Archives, UK. 2016. https://www.nationalarchives.gov.uk/education/empire/g3/cs4/background.htm

[26] Walsh, "Case Study 4 Background."

[27] Walsh, "Case Study 4 Background."

[28] Walsh, "Case Study 4 Background."

[29] Walsh, "Case Study 4 Background."

[30] Oral History from Barbara Inez Pletcher Quigley.

[31] Mary McCarthy's Trunk from Ireland, note dated 18 December 1966. Family Records.

[32] Barbara Inez Pletcher Quigley. Oral History.

[33] Sam B. Warner, *Streetcar Suburbs: The Process of Growth in Boston, 1870-1900*. 2nd ed.
(Cambridge, MA: Harvard University Press, 1978).

[34] Warner, *Streetcar Suburbs.*

[35] "Massachusetts, Birth Records, 1840-1915."Ancestry.com. [database on-line]. Provo, UT,
USA: Ancestry.com Operations, Inc., 2013. https://search.ancestry.com/cgi-bin/sse.dll?indiv=1&dbid=5062&h=851162&tid=&pid=&usePUB=true&_phsrc=FLW5&_phstart=successSource

[36] Ancestry.com. *U.S., World War I Draft Registration Cards, 1917-1918* [database on-line]. Provo, UT, USA: Ancestry.com Operations Inc, 2005. https://search.ancestry.com/cgi-bin/sse.dll?indiv=1&dbid=6482&h=17719487&tid=&pid=&usePUB=true&_phsrc=FLW8&_phstart=successSource

[37] "The Insurance Almanac and Encyclopedia: An Annual of Insurance Facts of 1917," 175.

[38] Ancestry.com. *Massachusetts, Marriage Index, 1901-1955 and 1966-1970* [database on-line]. Provo, UT, USA: Ancestry.com Operations, Inc., 2013. https://search.ancestry.com/cgi-bin/sse.dll?dbid=2966&h=4092153&indiv=try&o_vc=Record:OtherRecord&rhSource=1002

[39] Photo of Barbara Inez Pletcher in Nurse Uniform.

[40] Photo of Barbara Inez Pletcher in College.

[41] Oral History of Joan Quigley Newton.

[42] Letter to Quig from Bobby, 17 October 1952.

[43] Wedding Photo of Bobby and Quig. 25 October 1952.

[44] Photo of letters sent between Bobby and Quig over the years.

[45] "James Sarsfield Quigley." Find a Grave., https://www.findagrave.com/memorial/61927770/james-sarsfield-quigley

[46] Photo of Bobby Quigley and Toddler Joan, 1954.

[47] Photo of Quigley kids <Joan, Danny, Patrick, Bart>

[48] "James Sarsfield Quigley." Find a Grave.

https://www.findagrave.com/memorial/61927770/james-sarsfield-quigley
[49] Photo of Quig, Bobby, and Cara Quigley at the beach house.
[50] Hughes Family History. Personal Records. Chapter I.
[51] Hughes Family History. Personal Records. Chapter I.
[52] Hughes Family History. Chapter I, direct quote.
[53] Hughes Family History. Personal Records. Chapter I.
[54] Hughes Family History. Personal Records. Chapter I.
[55] Hughes Family History. Personal Records. Chapter I.
[56] John Loughery, "Dagger John: The Bishop Who Built Irish America," *The Irish Times*, 14 March 2018, https://www.irishtimes.com/culture/books/dagger-john-the-bishop-who-built-irish-america-1.3425444.
[57] Hughes Family History. Personal Records. Chapter I.
[58] Loughery, "Dagger John."
[59] Hughes Family History. Personal Records. Chapter I.
[60] Hughes Family History. Personal Records. Chapter II.
[61] Hughes Family History. Personal Records. Chapter II.
[62] Hughes Family History. Personal Records. Chapter VII.
[63] Hughes Family History. Personal Records. Chapter VII
[64] Hughes Family History. Personal Records. Chapter VII
[65] Hughes Family History. Personal Records. Chapter VII
[66] Photo of Bobby and Quig dancing.

Endnotes to Chapter 6

[1] Editors of Encyclopaedia Britannica, "What Is the Origin of the Term Holocaust?" *Encyclopædia Britannica*, 1 March 2020. https://www.britannica.com/story/what-is-the-origin-of-the-term-holocaust.
[2] Michael Berenbaum, "Kristallnacht," *Encyclopædia Britannica*, 13 February 2020. https://www.britannica.com/event/Kristallnacht.
[3] "Introduction to the Holocaust," 12 March 2018.
[4] Joseph Engle, *To Auschwitz And Back, 2018.*
[5] Engle, *To Auschwitz And Back*, 2018.
[6] Engle, *To Auschwitz And Back*, 2018.
[7] Engle, *To Auschwitz And Back*, 2018.
[8] Engle, *To Auschwitz And Back*, 2018.
[9] Engle, *To Auschwitz And Back*, 2018.
[10] Engle, *To Auschwitz And Back*, 2018.

[11] Engle, *To Auschwitz And Back*, 2018.
[12] Engle, *To Auschwitz And Back*, 2018.
[13] Engle, *To Auschwitz And Back*, 2018.
[14] "Nechama Pluznik," Interview, Charleston, 23 March 2020.
[15] "Nechama Pluznik," Interview, 23 March 2020.
[16] "Nechama Pluznik," Interview, 23 March 2020.
[17] "Nechama Pluznik," Interview, 23 March 2020.
[18] "Nechama Pluznik," Interview, 23 March 2020.
[19] "Nechama Pluznik," Interview, 23 March 2020.
[20] "Nechama Pluznik, Interview, 23 March 2020.
[21] "Nechama Pluznik, Interview, 23 March 2020.
[22] "Nechama Pluznik," Interview, 23 March 2020.
[23] "Nechama Pluznik," Interview, 23 March 2020.
[24] "Nechama Pluznik," Interview, 23 March 2020.
[25] "Nechama Pluznik," Interview, 23 March 2020.
[26] "Miki Pluznik Holocaust Experience," *Miki Pluznik Holocaust Experience*, n.d.
[27] "Miki Pluznik Holocaust Experience."
[28] "Miki Pluznik Holocaust Experience.".
[29] "Miki Pluznik Holocaust Experience."
[30] Lily Rothman, "Operation Finale's True Story and the Real Eichmann Trial" *Time*, 29 August 2018, time.com/5377670/operation-finale-adolf-eichmann-trial/.
[31] Rothman, "Operation Finale's True Story and the Real Eichmann Trial."
[32] "Miki Pluznik Holocaust Experience."
[33] "Miki Pluznik Holocaust Experience."
[34] Barbara Handler-Lachmann and Ulrich Schutt, "Memorial Site in Breitenau Archive and Exhibition of the Kassel Comprehensive University," *Memorial Site in Breitenau Archive and Exhibition of the Kassel Comprehensive University*, 1992.
[35] Handler-Lachmann and Schutt, "Memorial Site in Breitenau Archive and Exhibition of the Kassel Comprehensive University."
[36] "Riga," United States Holocaust Memorial Museum. United States Holocaust Memorial Museum, 1 March 2020. https://encyclopedia.ushmm.org/content/en/article/riga.
[37] Michael Tarm, "Panel Examines Latvian Nazis." *The Associated Press*, n.d.

[38] Tarm, "Panel Examines Latvian Nazis."
[39] Tarm, "Panel Examines Latvian Nazis."
[40] Tarm, "Panel Examines Latvian Nazis."
[41] "Riga," United States Holocaust Memorial Museum.
[42] Tarm, "Panel Examines Latvian Nazis."
[43] "Meir Pluznik Holocaust Experience." *Meir Pluznik Holocost Experience*, n.d.
[44] "Meir Pluznik Holocaust Experience."
[45] "Meir Pluznik Holocaust Experience."
[46] "Daniel Holocaust Experience," *Daniel Holocaust Experience*, n.d.
[47] "Daniel Holocaust Experience."
[48] "Daniel Holocaust Experience."
[49] "Nechama Pluznik," Interview, 23 March 2020.